The eye of the needle

For my mother

with love

The eye *of the* needle

Roy K. McCloughry

Inter-Varsity Press

INTER-VARSITY PRESS
38 De Montfort Street, Leicester LE1 7GP, England

First published 1990

British Library Cataloguing in Publication Data
McCloughry, Roy
The eye of the needle.
1. Society – Christian viewpoints
I. Title
261

ISBN 0-85110-685-4

Set in 10/11pt Baskerville by Avocet Robinson, Buckingham
Printed in Great Britain by Richard Clay Ltd, Bungay

Inter-Varsity Press is the book-publishing division of the Universities and Colleges Christian Fellowship (formerly the Inter-Varsity Fellowship), a student movement linking Christian Unions in universities and colleges throughout the United Kingdom and the Republic of Ireland, and a member movement of the International Fellowship of Evangelical Students. For information about local and national activities write to UCCF, 38 De Montfort Street, Leicester LE1 7GP.

Contents

FOREWORD

I have enjoyed Roy McCloughry's friendship for a number of years, and I specially admired his leadership during the six years that he served as Director of the Shaftesbury Project, which was founded to promote Christian involvement in society. Already we have reason to be grateful for his writings on AIDS, debt, unemployment and Christian social action; now we welcome his first full-length book. He modestly calls it 'a personal statement'. But it is more than that. It is a thoughtful, passionate, prophetic call to the church to be an authentic witness to God's kingdom of justice and love.

I am impressed by the range of topics which Roy covers. He seems to be equally at home whether he is discussing politics or economics, church or state, welfare, wisdom, worship or lifestyle. Yet these topics are not handled in isolation from one another. For he is determined to break down the false distinction between the sacred and the secular, and to develop a true integration of evangelism and social responsibility, spirituality and justice, prayer and action.

Competent lay theologian that he is, Roy McCloughry's starting-point is the character of God as revealed in Christ and in Scripture. It is who God is that determines what we should be. Moreover, Roy's resolve to submit to Scripture rightly leads him into the Old Testament as well as the New, while at the same time he affirms the centrality for all our thinking of Christ's cross.

His persuasive, positive summons to us to be a transformed and distinctive people, and both to manifest and to disseminate the values of the kingdom of God, necessitates a frank exposure of contemporary idolatries, especially of personal narcissism and of economic self-interest. All political ideologies, being human constructs, are flawed. They are never more than a mixture of good and evil, of visionary idealism and crooked reality; only the kingdom of God is perfect.

I am grateful for Roy McCloughry's honesty. There is nothing slick or superficial about this book. He addresses real questions, struggles to find Christian answers, maintains his integrity in the argument and, where necessary, confesses his own perplexity.

His style flows smoothly and he has a gift for aphorisms. Here is a small selection: 'we have a welfare state because we have failed at being a welfare society'; 'our style of life is intimately related to our view of death'; 'because Jesus was confident of his status as a Son, he was set free to be a servant'; and 'our world needs to be astonished by love rather than sickened by evil'. I hope that these will whet the reader's appetite for more.

John Stott
September 1989

PREFACE

Thanks are due to many people for their help during the writing of this book. It was put together during my time as the Director of the Shaftesbury Project (now Christian Impact) and I am very grateful to the Trustees and Council of the Project for their support from 1982 to 1988. Thanks too to Kath Semple and Jacky Draper for their efficient word-processing and to Debbie Watmough for help with research. The book was completed after my move to the Kingdom Trust and I am very grateful to its Trustees for their tremendous support and for their provision of many facilities which made the writing of this book much easier.

In particular I am indebted to those churches which support the Trust both financially and prayerfully. All Souls, Langham Place; St. Peter's, Farnborough; St. Nicholas', Nottingham and St. Paul's and St. George's, Edinburgh together with many other individuals, provided the means and the encouragement necessary for this book to be completed. In many senses this book belongs to them.

Mike LeRoy, John Wyatt, James Catford, Martyn Eden, John Stott and Helen McCloughry all read the manuscript and I am very grateful to them for their astute comments. Jean McCloughry made important stylistic comments which were very helpful. I am especially grateful to 'Uncle John' for providing a foreword. None of the above are responsible for the many inadequacies of the text.

My family has given me wonderful support not only during the writing of this book, but also during the many times when I was away preaching and lecturing. Thank you, not only to Helen without whose loving support I would have given it all up long ago, but also to Joanna, Elizabeth and Lauren who livened up many a dull moment and provided their own special magic.

The book is really a personal statement about some of the key issues which face us as Christians as we approach the next millennium. It has no claims to be 'academic' or 'authoritative', though some readers might find parts of it denser than others. I hope that some will find it an encouragement to see the modern world as a mission field.

Those who wished for more practical guidance in chapter thirteen on how to take action will find it in a small book entitled *Taking action* (Frameworks), which may be regarded as a sequel to that chapter. It provides many practical ideas about how to take effective action in the local, national and international community.

My hope is that God will be able to use this book in some small way to break down some of the walls we have erected in our thinking and help us to bring together a more biblical approach to spirituality with a passion for justice.

Roy McCloughry
Lady Bay, May 1989

CHAPTER ONE

THE EMPEROR'S NEW CLOTHES

In the nineteenth century the problem was that God is dead; in the twentieth century the problem is that man is dead.

ERICH FROMM

Here we are, we're alone in the universe, there's no God, it just seems that it all began by something as simple as light striking on a piece of rock. And here we are. We've only got ourselves. Somehow, we've just got to make a go of it. We've only ourselves.

JOHN OSBORNE

What are the implications of being a Christian in the modern world? An adequate answer to this question is vital if we are to engage in mission and dialogue with that world. As Christians we cannot live as if culture and modernity were somehow neutral and had no influence over us. Nor should we be surprised when people no longer understand the religious language we often use.

If we are to relate our faith in an invisible God to the demands of a materialistic world we must be aware of the culture we live in. It does not share our priorities as Christians and it can be deeply suspicious of Christian involvement.

Yet if there is one thing that we have had to learn in recent years, it is that the Christian faith is cultural as well as personal or spiritual.

Those who cannot or will not recognize the extent to which patterns of worship and belief have been influenced by the modern world will be hampered in encountering that world in mission as well as in dealing with its infiltration of their own life and witness.

Shying away from such an encounter is understandable. Those who grapple with the problems we face as a global community have an impossible task. Christians who are committed to 'the right and the good' usually prefer neat solutions to problems which can be clearly articulated. We are happiest when an important social or ethical problem has a right and a wrong answer. We can then support the one against the other. We are least happy when urgent and important issues seem to have no resolution in terms which are clearly good. We recognize that, in such situations, Christians might, after having studied the Scriptures and searched their own consciences, come down on different sides of the debate. This prospect of disagreement between Christians fills us with foreboding.

Some would rather we did not get involved in the first place. These Christians are 'risk-averse', to use a phrase borrowed from the language of economics. They would rather stay with the traditional agenda than engage in dialogue with the modern world. Such a defensive position is understandable. All kinds of people are looking for shelter from the fall-out of the crisis-ridden world we live in. The proliferation of cults, the rise of therapy, the pursuit of materialism all promise refuge for those who wish to turn their back on the world and deny responsibility for it.

The winds of change

But over the last twenty-five years things have begun to change. We have begun to realize that when the church was born on the day of Pentecost its mission was not to throw words at the problems of a needy world and then retreat to safety. When the Holy Spirit came, Christ himself was given to the church. So the difference between Christianity and every other proselytizing creed is that we do not offer words alone – *we offer Christ himself*.

Our world has become convinced that only those things that can be handled with the five senses can be trusted. The mission of the body of Christ is to make Christ visible to a world for whom he is invisible. This must mean not only preaching words *about* Christ but demonstrating Christ's love, justice, mercy and hope in a needy world.

This cannot be done if we confine our activities within the four walls of a church building. The world is crying out for a demonstration of the consequences of faith in this invisible God. What we have realized in recent years is that people of faith must be risk-takers. They are to be in the market-place, in the storm, where the action is, demonstrating the difference Christ makes and bringing Christ to those who are suffering.

God calls his people to be 'in the world but not of it'. Those of us who have been born into the modern world are faced with an exhilarating yet daunting challenge. For this is a world beset by crisis. It is a world which denies the very existence of the Creator-God, yet it is a world which has released powers which appear to be out of control. Everywhere commentators are saying 'We cannot continue as we are.'

We face crises in the environmental, economic, nuclear, social and personal spheres. As this time world leaders are needed to portray a social vision of depth and spiritual insight which can unite and motivate people to overcome these problems. Instead we are being sold a justification of material self-gratification which is remarkable only for its arid shallowness.

A prophetic vision

The Bible tells us that 'without a vision the people perish'. Our generation is withering for the lack of just such a vision. Who will bring it if not the church of Jesus Christ? We have realized nearly too late that behind the economic, environmental and social crises of our day there are spiritual realities.

The prophets of the Old Testament could take the events of history and show the people the hand of God at work.

> What concerns the prophet is the human event as a divine experience. History to us is the record of human experience; to the prophet it is the record of God's experience.[1]

The prophets knew that each crisis was a potential turning point, a positive opportunity for people to return to God. In our age we face a similar challenge to convince the world about Jesus Christ.

The prophets would first expose the idolatry of their day and show how it had led to oppression and disobedience. Having exposed it, they would then start to rebuild the people's faith in God. They would show that such belief had consequences for how the people should live. The prophets would then lead them back to becoming a holy and distinctive people.

What the prophets did we need to do again. We need to do it for those who do not believe in God, to show that he is relevant and authoritative in the modern world. We need to do it for ourselves, for sadly we have been infiltrated by unbelief at crucial points. We need to recover our courage and our belief in the adequacy of God if we are to be risk-takers and people of faith.

Lord of all

Our ability to view the world prophetically is hampered by the fact that we have a tendency to restrict God's influence to religious territory. We have convinced ourselves that, because we do not live in Old Testament times when prophets ordained by God called the people back to the covenant, we cannot exercise a prophetic ministry in the world. Yet it is we whom the Holy Spirit uses to 'convince the world of sin, righteousness and judgment'. God has only one kingdom and it is we who are witnesses to its existence. It is our challenge to the self-absorbed folly of the world to declare that it is possible, by God's grace, to 'follow another King, one Jesus'. To speak incisively into the modern world, with the words of God, by the Spirit of God, for the glory of God, is to exercise a prophetic ministry. Yet those who are recognized by others to have such gifts will never apply the label of 'prophet' to themselves. The difference between the prophets of old and those who speak out in our day is that in those days God called men and women to be prophets and prophetesses. Since the giving of the Spirit it is our message which is 'prophetic'. No individual living today has the right to the authority of those prophets who revealed the very heart of God. Yet where there is truth, courage and boldness to speak into the contemporary world, there is authority enough for God's word to be heard and heeded once again.

It is therefore ironic and sad that so often we divide the world into the sacred and the secular. We seek God in the sacred and neglect to look for him in those areas of life which we have pronounced to be 'secular'. In recent decades there has been an increasing awareness that, by doing this, it is we who restrict the Lordship of Jesus Christ. He is the Creator-God. For him there is no difference between the sacred and the secular. He upholds all things by the word of his power. There is no place we can go in this world where God is not there before us; no activity we undertake which cannot be related to him; no job which he does not work at alongside us.

Because of this, there is hope in the inner city and on the depressed outer housing estates. Because of this there is dignity in the sweat-shop and in the monotony of the assembly line. He is Lord of the arts, of sport, of science and of politics. Even our technology and science should take their place as his tools in our hands and reflect the priorities of his world.

It is this God that the modern world rejects. Instead, the world we live in is convinced of its own cleverness. It is a world of deep paradoxes and heart-rending ironies. We can put men on the moon, but we cannot protect our children from child abuse. We can fertilize human embryos in test-tubes, but we permit the silent holocaust of abortion to continue. We can bring people divided by vast distances together by satellite, only to separate next-door neighbours by a careless insult about the colour of their skin. We are capable of great scientific achievements but consider science and technology to be a monument to our own expertise and a demonstration that we have come of age without the need for God.

The modern world clothes itself in its own cleverness. But for anyone who sees from God's perspective it struts around naked and deluded like the emperor of the children's fable. As the church exposes the idolatry which has led to such delusion its aim is not to ridicule but to restore.

So our starting point is a critique of contemporary idolatry. Idolatry never went out of fashion; it just went up-market.

CHAPTER TWO

IDOLS OF THE MIND

•

To knock over an idol you must first get off your knees.

R. H. TAWNEY

To commit idolatry is to live in a shrinking world. Human beings can remain fully human and explore what it means to be human only if they are constantly being stretched by trying to understand the mind of the transcendent Creator-God. Those of us who have settled for less because it is easier or more convenient may not see ourselves as idolaters, but that is what we are. To be satisfied with anything less than 'true truth' is to deny certain basic facts about the universe which are available to everybody.

In his letter to the Romans, Paul states that societies come under the judgment of God when they deny certain essential facts about God which are 'plain to them'.[1]

> For since the creation of the world God's invisible qualities – his eternal power and divine nature – have been clearly seen, being understood from what has been made, so that men are without excuse.[2]

People divide into two camps. There are those for whom life provokes faith and reverence for the Creator-God and those who, in Paul's own words, 'neither glorify God nor give thanks to him'. This universal act of repressing the most basic awareness of God has led to a search not only for alternative explanations of the origins of the universe but also for alternative objects of worship.

Paul continues by remarking that God is the sustainer of wisdom.

> Their thinking became futile and their foolish hearts were darkened. Although they claimed to be wise, they became fools and exchanged the glory of the immortal God for images made to look like mortal man and birds and animals and reptiles.[3]

In the name of wisdom and sophisticated thinking, people become idolatrous. It is not that they always worship evil and are, therefore, overtly evil themselves. Paul comments:

> They exchanged the truth of God for a lie, and worshipped and served created things rather than the Creator . . .[4]

For these reasons the Bible does not see people who are taken up with other things as innocent. It represents them as chasing foolishness dressed up as wisdom. The prophet Isaiah comments on those who take a piece of wood and burn half of it to heat their stew and make an idol out of the other half. Of such people the prophet says, 'No one stops to think.' Such actions are the product of 'a deluded heart'.[5]

> They know nothing, they understand nothing; their eyes are plastered over so that they cannot see, and their minds closed so that they cannot understand.[6]

What is idolatry?

There is, among those who have rejected God, a universal drive to replace him. For instance, modern life is full of our attempts to find ways of dealing with the anxiety and guilt which we now carry because we do not believe in God. Such guilt cannot drive us as sinners towards a God who will forgive us, since he no longer exists.

More often we focus on some alternative idea or therapy which we can manipulate. We still wish our anxiety and guilt to be taken away. We therefore look for a new philosophy which tells us that they do not exist, or a new interest to distract us from them. We will do anything to avoid the implications of returning to a belief in a holy Creator-God.

> In the light of the demand to be holy, we seek something close at hand and manageable. And so we fabricate some object – or project on to some other object or person – the worship we owe to the Transcendent. Feelings of guilt now can become more negotiable in terms of payments we make to our 'idol'.[7]

So idolatry involves first making and then worshipping a God created by people instead of worshipping the true God. David Lyon, the sociologist, comments:

> . . . idolatry is the investing of trust and hope in that which is unworthy of them, and incapable of rewarding them.[8]

Idolatry occurs when people live lives according to a creed based on a deliberate distortion of the truth, or when they passively accept the *status quo* and do not bother to challenge its distortions. In both cases people are satisfied with partial and mechanistic explanations of events which other cultures (including our own in times past) would have seen as requiring a 'God framework' in order to be complete.

For instance, both socialism and capitalism are often treated as complete and satisfactory frameworks for thinking about the world (even though they are competing world views). Yet both of these systems of thought are partial and incomplete.

But rather than seeing socialism, capitalism or democracy as incomplete and provisional we often elevate them to the status of absolutes by which we judge the rest of life.

Serving good or serving God?

Family life, too, can come to be regarded as sacred. Sociologist Tony Walter points out that Christians are often very good at providing a critique of materialism as idolatry but are strangely blind when they have replaced God by the 'goods' of work or the family.

> . . . rather than being simply part of the good life, modern romantic and parental love claims to be the good life.[9]

There is no room, therefore, for complacency. There is a constant tendency to replace the worship of God with the practice of good.

When we use sacred language for anything besides God, we are often expressing our need for ideals which are above the normal humdrum of everyday life. By projecting sacred language onto these things we are packaging them to make them appear worthy of our attention.

The beautiful models who pose as the feminine 'ideal' in the glossy magazines do not fall out of bed that way in the morning. Significantly we refer to them as being 'made up' (by which we mean that they have applied cosmetics to their faces), but they are made up in a much more fundamental sense. They are an 'image'. We are all too ready to believe our own make-believe because we need to idealize things outside our own immediate experience.

A distorted image

The force of idolatry is found in its ability to distort or misdirect our strongest desires while persuading us that what we are doing is essentially good. Most people who idolize riches claim that they only want to be 'comfortable'. Those who idolize fashion are those most often heard to exclaim with dismay, 'I haven't a thing to wear.'

We are masters and mistresses of self-justification, finding extenuating circumstances in our lives which do not appear to exist in the lives of others. Because of this we deflect criticism away from ourselves and are more adept at thinking morally and ethically about the problems of others than about our own vulnerabilities.

When God's people succumb to idolatry it is always because there is something about God which they are not prepared to accept. This gradually distorts their perception of God, which in turn affects their obedience and leads to their becoming a community which does not faithfully reflect the true God.

Although a church may say that it is preaching the gospel, another message may be communicated much more strongly by the way the church is living. A church in an impoverished inner-city area which concentrates on its organ fund need not wonder why it has no success in mission. Its message is quite plain: organs matter more than people.

We become like the object of our worship. A materialistic church which is not facing up to its responsibility to the poor, will not worship the God of justice nor will it welcome preaching on the subject.

As Ezekiel found, those whose hearts are set on 'unjust gain' may listen to the preacher, but he is no more than an entertainer and the message lasts about as far as Sunday lunch. Such people do not 'sit under the word', struggling to become obedient to it. They would rather discuss the merits or demerits of the preacher. Such a widespread practice is a sign that something is seriously wrong.[10]

It is therefore important that we be aware of the culture in which we live. Unless we become acutely sensitive to its weaknesses and its strengths, we shall not be able to separate them from our own. The more Christianity adapts to the culture which surrounds it, the less it is able to encounter or challenge it. The process by which idolatry takes hold in a society has several distinctive stages which it is vital to recognize.

The first sign: the death of divinity

Susan Sontag, the distinguished American literary critic and philosopher, writes,

> . . . of all possible crimes which an entire culture can commit, the one most difficult to bear psychologically, is deicide. We live in a society whose way of life testifies to the thoroughness with which the deity has been dispatched, but philosophers, writers, men of conscience everywhere squirm under the burden. For it is a far simpler matter to plot and commit a crime than it is to live with it afterwards.[11]

One of the most significant milestones in this process came with the advent of the eighteenth-century Enlightenment. This was a turning point in the development of modern culture. Of course the thinking of the Enlightenment did not appear out of nowhere, nor did any golden age precede it as some Christian writers imply, but it did usefully provide a fulcrum between medieval and modern cultures.

The impact of the Enlightenment has been discussed at length by Lesslie Newbigin in his books *The Other Side of 1984* and *Foolishness to the Greeks*. In his opinion what happened was that a change occurred in what was seen as a satisfactory explanation of events. A dissatisfaction with dogmatic theological explanations grew, especially since they seemed to be at odds with the new 'science'. With the rise of science, 'true explanations' of phenomena were emerging. The light was dawning. Hence the word 'Enlightenment'.

But the new science did not offer a view of the world which was related to God. Quite the opposite. Lesslie Newbigin gives a helpful analogy by recounting his own early experience in India.

> One of the first things I did on arrival in India was to be involved in a bus accident which laid me off for two years. How to 'explain' it? The Indian pastor said: 'It is the will of God.' A Hindu would have said: 'The karma of your former lives has caught up with you.' In some cultures the explanation would be that an enemy had put a curse on me. If I, as an 'enlightened' European had said that it was all because the brakes were not working properly, that would have been – for the others – no explanation at all. It would have been simply a re-statement of what had to be explained. To speak of an 'explanation' is to speak of the ultimate framework of axioms and assumptions by means of which one 'makes sense of things'.[12]

Scientists became the interpreters of the new age. Instead of the priests explaining the mysteries of God to the people, scientists 'explained' that these were no longer mysteries but simply processes of cause and effect in a rational world. Only things which were observable were admissible as evidence. Since God could not be observed he was replaced either by a weakly defined deism, or at a much later point by the idea of 'chance'.

Human reason was elevated as the tool which could unlock all mysteries. The inevitability of progress replaced original sin. Economics became divorced from ethics and religious influence. Society, which had been based on responsibilities and duties within the community, became focused on the rights of the individual.

Intolerable burdens were placed on the state since one could no longer rely on the judgment of God in an afterlife which probably didn't exist. An invisible God could not be trusted to right the wrongs of human history after death. It was important then that sufficient power was given to the state in order that it could oversee the distribution of penalties and later of benefits in society.

Yet at the same time this revolution of thinking was responsible for much that is good and beneficial in modern society. The right of the individual to think for herself, the benefits to society of modern science and economics have all conferred on us a higher standard of living and health-care. It has also resulted in a degree of understanding about our world which is without parallel in human history.

But at the heart of the Enlightenment, as Lesslie Newbigin points out, was an insidious change for the worse. We now accepted partial and mechanistic explanations of phenomena which had previously required a God framework. Out of this ferment came the works of Marx, Darwin and Freud with their opposition to the Christian world-view and their alternative explanations of economic, biological and personal life.

We became impressed by our own abilities. This was especially true in the field of technology. The insatiable desire to see what 'could' be done began to overrun traditional guidelines about what 'should' be done. We have arrived at a point where the problem is that our technical ability is outstripping our ethical ability. New medical technologies, for instance, not only solve problems, but also create them. We are thankful for life support systems, but under what condition should they be switched off? The irony is that the very revolution of thinking which led to this technological revolution has reduced our capacity to use it by denying us the Christian framework for our thought.

It is vital that Christians enter these fields and challenge the conventional wisdom of today. Christians are called to be restorers of perspective. This calling is not restricted to missionaries and clergy. The mother, the teacher and the unemployed person are also called to challenge their worlds in the name of Christ. The idolatry of the family, education and work will otherwise continue to tie our society in knots.

This an exciting commission, but it can be fulfilled only if we ourselves can see clearly. If idolatry has infiltrated the church then radical changes will be needed if we are not to be the 'blind leading the blind' or 'the bland leading the bland'.

It may be that some of us are like the man whom Jesus healed at Bethsaida. After Jesus had laid hands on him once, he could see 'men like trees walking'. Perhaps like him we need 'a second touch' for our sight to be fully restored.

The second sign: the myth of normality

Once a culture has put God to death, it then attempts to behave as if nothing has happened. As Susan Sontag pointed out, it is this part of the exercise which is most difficult to live with. If it is true that we are made by God, for God, then the impact of the death of God will be considerable, in both personal and social terms.

Those who believe in what they have done will present it as a liberation. God (or as they will say 'the idea of God') was just a crutch to lean on, a teddy bear to cuddle so that we would not have to face up to what is going on in the world. Just how far this has proceeded can be seen in a quote by a distinguished thinker, Professor Charles Taylor:

> There are certain very important, you might say almost spiritual goals or ideals or values which arose in the west. And I'll name just two which are, I think, behind modern society – a certain idea of freedom, and the notion that the centre of life, of the purpose of life, of the meaning of life, is to be found in what I want to call 'ordinary life' itself, that is the life of the family, the life of production. This distinguishes modern civilisation from most previous civilisations, which have had a notion that there is something beyond ordinary life, some higher type of activity or perhaps otherworldly type of worship which is the centre of human life, which is what human life is about.[13]

The most fundamental form of idolatry in the modern world is the belief that there is something called 'ordinary life', which does not need to refer to God and which is 'normal'. It is a view subscribed to by the majority of 'ordinary decent people' whose major belief is that God is unnecessary. This belief, which they regard as no-belief, is regarded as harmless, since they are not evil and merely wish to 'get on with their lives'.

For many people the idea of 'ordinary life' is focused on survival through the many pressures that life brings them. For them it is no longer the case that life is an adventure or an exploration of God's world. It has become a struggle to protect themselves from the many influences which would seek to take them over: divorce, loneliness, neurosis, failure, illness or mere emptiness in the midst of plenty or want.

Living as if God does not exist leaves us with the routines of life expressed through the family and with accumulation of things and experiences. It is easy for this attitude to infiltrate the church. Christians can live a parallel to 'ordinary life' by adding the word 'religious' to it: 'ordinary religious life'.

Normal Christians or normative Christians?

In this approach to Christianity, which defies all denominational boundaries and divisions based on doctrine, our expectations of God are confined to our Christian routines. We are guided by what is *normal* rather than what is *normative*. The Bible provides the general direction for Christian behaviour as well as much of the correct language. But our lives are lived in imitation of *each other*. So normality rules. This 'myth of normality' holds many dangers for the unwary. The Christian life can become just another routine. We are thus left with the convention of Christianity without its power.

In my own experience this difference between living 'normatively' and living 'normally' is seen most markedly when working with young Christians. I remember working with a group of young adults who had recently become Christians. During five years with that group (whose membership was constantly turning over), I noticed the same pattern emerging. Immediately after they had become Christians they were extremely enthusiastic. Many of them felt no hesitation about sharing their new faith with others. They read the Scriptures and prayed for long periods and were very willing to accept Christian teaching and to attempt to put it into practice.

After the first few months things began to change. You could say that 'the honeymoon period was over' or 'they were settling down'. What was actually happening was that they had woken up to the fact that other Christians who were older in the faith and therefore 'more mature' were not always as enthusiastic about evangelism, Bible study and prayer as they were. The 'normal' Christian life became the 'average' Christian life. They began to be satisfied with mediocrity.

The fallacy of control

The cult of normality is the cult of the middle class. The peace which reigns over our suburbs is carefully cultivated. It is a peace which allows individuals to pursue their own goals in privacy. Money gives us power to reduce uncertainty in our lives. We can lock our doors in the knowledge that our dues are paid and we are nobody's debtor. Nothing can disturb our domestic equilibrium and we are thankful for it. The dangerous element in this can be summed up in one word, *control*.

Those of us who have the power over our lives are in great danger from one of the greatest blessings of this life: the ability to make our own decisions. Life can continue its regular rhythm because we are in control. It is we who determine what we do and what is done to us. As the domain of control increases, so will the tendency to ask God's opinion of decisions which we have already taken.

The temptation for the powerful person is to limit God to those areas where he can do the least harm and not upset the *status quo*. Such behaviour is closely allied to the view that Christianity is about happiness and that God wants us to be happy. The message of the cross is downgraded into a contentless cipher in this view. The Christ of the cross is not happy, yet he is perfectly fulfilling the Father's will. The place of pain and suffering in the will of God for our lives is something we find difficult to cope with because we have become used to controlling our own lives according to the 'happiness criterion'.

Every Sunday preachers exhort their congregations to 'take up their cross and follow Christ'. This is heard by many in the congregation as 'support your local church', something which they are only too pleased to do, since it fits quite well into their view of normality. They are prepared to do anything 'for God' which fits within their definition of living a normal, regular life. The idea of breaking such a pattern is unthinkable for many people.

We are also exhorted to 'love our enemies', to which our response is 'But I have no enemies.' We, therefore, remain unsure about what to do with this teaching and determine to live life much as before.

The problem is that our expectations of what God *will* do in our lives begin to shrink – closely followed by our belief in what God *can* do. To experience God in this way is to reduce Christianity to a religious product of which we are a consumer, a therapy for which we are a client or an ideology of which we are a supporter. It is far removed from biblical Christianity. In Susan Sontag's words it is 'piety without content'.

The third sign: the loss of identity

In Exodus 33 we find Moses in conversation with God about the idolatry of Israel. Moses was worried that God would not continue to be present with his people, since they had spurned him by committing idolatry. His question was,

> 'How will anyone know that you are pleased with me and with your people unless you go with us? What else

will distinguish me and your people from all the other people on the face of the earth?'[14]

Moses knew that the only thing which distinguished Israel from any other people was the presence of God. Their entire life as a nation rested on the fact that 'Yahweh was their King'. It was his character which was reflected in their laws and economic life. His mercy and justice were the source of theirs, his liberating them from slavery was the source of their common brotherhood.

If God had not gone with Israel then their life together would have been a hollow set of conventions. God's presence led to distinctiveness in his people.

The strategy of the church

If Christians merge into the background, this removes the 'offence' of Christianity. Over the twentieth century we have seen the process of secularization rob religion of much of its power in society. Instead of religion being a belief in an objective 'God who is there', it is now seen as a subjective expression of human desire that such a God *should* exist. Some people are seen as needing God to exist. This is regarded as a personal weakness by a world which believes in autonomy as a sign of strength. Since people find meaning in life through sport, sex, art or science, religion is now seen as one source of 'comfort' among many.

This approach to religion as one option among many has put Christians on the defensive. Peter Berger, the sociologist of religion, points out that there are two strategies that can be adopted in such a situation.

A defensive strategy. The first is a strategy of defence. This forms a sub-culture composed of people who still believe the assumptions which are under fire from the modern sceptical world. They seek to maintain the faith until such time as society returns to belief again. The problem is that they are not immune to what is going on outside. Media culture quickly adopts a sceptical position where doubt is elevated to sophistication and faith is denigrated as naivety. It is difficult for this not to have an effect on believers. In their determination to retain the truth they may well also enshrine elements of their subculture as well. This is how, for example, wearing hats in church can become an eleventh commandment.

The strategy of accommodation. The opposite defence is one of accommodation. Here people are willing to give up certain things by negotiation in order to be thought of as modern.

> The more moderate liberal position may be characterized as a bargaining procedure with secularized consciousness: 'We'll give you the virgin birth but we'll keep the resurrection'; 'You can have the Jesus of history, but we'll hold on to the Christ of the apostolic faith'; and so on.[15]

Others would go further and would give up any attempt to believe in the supernatural. These are the secular theologians whose work is often indistinguishable from other philosophies. Berger comments about them,

> The particular paradox in engaging in the discipline of divinity while denying the divine is hardly likely to recommend itself to many people for very long.[16]

The *defensive* strategy leads to an emphasis on authority at the expense of relevance, while the *accommodation* strategy leads to an emphasis on relevance at the expense of authority. In contrast to both, we are called to be *integrated but distinctive* in the modern world.

The proliferation of choice

Even within the evangelical church we have been affected by the fact that we live in a secularized society. A society in which a proliferation of choices, still retaining the Christian label, is increasingly apparent.

A bewildering number of different church groups call themselves biblical Christians and yet believe fundamentally different things about the role of the church in the world, the work of the Holy Spirit, the nature of Christian guidance and other important issues.

Of course we can say very positively that all this is part of the richness and diversity of Christian experience. But there is a problem. In his book *The Gravedigger File*[17] Os Guinness portrays it as a smorgasbord. I was introduced to these in Sweden. A table was groaning with food of every description (and some which defied description!). I moved down the table taking a little bit of this and a little bit of that. The only thing which determined what was on my plate was my own personal taste. Os Guinness remarks that many of us treat our Christian faith in a similar way. The options are so vast that we take 'a little bit of this and a little bit of that'.

We become dabblers. Because of this our Christianity is losing its corporate nature and becoming a collection of individualistic interpretations. We choose those types of church, worship style, doctrinal emphasis which are our 'cup of tea' and we say 'Now that's my kind of Christianity.' It is a short step from that to saying 'Now that's my kind of God.'

What has happened is that the fashion for equality between world views has infiltrated the church. If some can deny the resurrection and still call themselves Christians, can't we go just one step further and tolerate (or even better accept) the beliefs of those decent people who just cannot bring themselves to believe in God?

So we seem to be pushed between different fads and fancies. Our blend of Christianity is determined by our personal taste. What is needed is a corporate commitment to the objective truth of the Scriptures. What does the 'historic Christian faith' stand for and who speaks for it? Fragmentation undermines the authority of the gospel in the world and dissipates its power. As a result, the world continues its search for truth elsewhere.

The painful truth for Christians to face is that we have chosen those parts of the Christian faith and of the character of God with which we feel at home and have neglected the rest. Is this not a form of idolatry?

Israel compromised its faith and fashioned an idol which did not make the moral and ethical demands which Yahweh made of them. As soon as they did this they ceased to be a remarkable people and began to reflect the unsavoury characteristics of the idol they had chosen for themselves.

Our idolatry is not that of overt evil. It is the *idolatry of the mediocre*. Notice, for instance, how tolerance has become a 'Christian' virtue in itself without any reference to what we are meant to be tolerant *of*. But Christians are called to be committed to a truth which makes strict moral and ethical demands. It is one thing to love others who show the same weaknesses and sins as we do. It is quite another to tolerate those who call sinfulness 'normality'.

Many with responsibility in the church, including many theologians, have so hedged the gospel round with caveats that it no longer seems strong enough to resist the secularizing influence of the world.

A timid message about tolerance and a sentimental attitude towards love have made us into a culture which lacks respect for truth and is unable to counter evil.

The idolatry of which Paul wrote in Romans 1 was that of a society which was rotten to the core. Those things which should have caused shame were deemed to be normal practice. Christians who live passively in such a culture find themselves under its influence and often on the retreat.

A routine Christianity in which God never demands much from us, and in which little besides attending church distinguishes us from those around us, keeps going because people compare their Christian lives with those of other Christians rather than with God's norms. Such a view of normality fits neatly into the space which the world is prepared to allow us for the sake of its own convenience.

It is not necessarily times of crisis and persecution that provide the greatest threat to the existence of the church as the distinctive people of God. Persecution often (though sadly not always) causes Christians to forget their differences and to fight together with great courage for the fundamentals of their faith. *The greatest threat comes with those periods of 'normality' which are accompanied by material affluence and during which the church is tempted to adopt a set of normal routines which peacefully coexist side by side with the world.*

CHAPTER THREE

NOT WAVING BUT DROWNING?

Nobody heard him, the dead man,
But still he lay moaning:
I was much further out than you thought
And not waving but drowning.

Poor chap, he always loved larking
And now he's dead
It must have been too cold for him
his heart gave way
They said.

Oh, no, no, no, it was too cold always
(Still the dead one lay moaning)
I was much too far out all my life
And not waving but drowning.

STEVIE SMITH[1]

When people create idols they are asserting their own will over God's will. Each idol made is an act of rebellion, a monument to the self. Humanity worships itself and its own choices as it bows down. It elevates the self to the status of God. Any tendency to romanticize or glory in the self is directly at odds with Christianity since Christ calls his disciples to find life in *losing* the self.[2]

It is because of this that psychologist Paul Vitz comments that, 'in religious terms selfist humanism is just another example of idolatrous narcissism'.[3]

The modern tendency to see the self as a pool of resources or even as Vitz says 'a potential paradise' is, therefore, fraught with problems for the Christian. But Christians cannot ignore a critique of such idolatry, feeling that it does not apply to them. It may well be that such an attitude has also shaped modern Christianity.

Psychologists and psychoanalysts claim that the major personality disorder which they are currently treating is narcissism. Similarly sociologists have taken the patterns of clinical behaviour peculiar to the narcissist and are applying them to the behaviour of Western society as a whole.

The disorder takes its name from the Greek legend of Narcissus, son of Cephalus the river god. The nymph Echo was in love with him but he rejected her love and despite the warnings of friends became fascinated with his own reflection in a pool of water. One day he leant over to kiss his reflection and drowned in the pool.

Narcissists and egoists

This story has become a picture of the worship of the self. It was Freud who first used it to describe those people who seemed to be obsessed with the self. So prevalent has it become that we are told that it is 'the characteristic personality disorder of our day'. Not only is it seen in the analyst's consulting room but it is present in milder forms in the lives of many of us. It is important to grapple with its implications because, having emerged over the last hundred years, it indicates how the rise of modernity has affected us personally.

The most important element of narcissism is that although it focuses on the self, it is diametrically opposed to egoism, though it is still ego-*centric*. When we think of self-worship we instinctively think of egoists. Such people do not care what others think of them and they see the world as theirs to conquer. They are imperialists who delight in putting their stamp on everything. They are the J. R. Ewings of this world.

Narcissists are precisely the opposite. They, too, focus on the self but they have a pathetically inadequate sense of self. Whereas egoists impose the self, narcissists are on a quest to discover the self. They are in constant need of the affirmation and admiration of others and when such admiration declines they may become depressed or even paranoic. They are, therefore, dependent on others and are desperately insecure in themselves.

Self-absorption

Technically narcissism is an inability to distinguish between the self and the outside world. Narcissus drowned because he failed to distinguish his own reflection from the presence of a second person. In the place of healthy independence and personal security, narcissists have a constant need to be told that they matter and are important to somebody. They may be unable to divorce themselves from the impression they are making on others. This in turn may give rise to grandiose flights of fancy in which people project a 'public persona' which they feel is acceptable to the rest of the world. Privately they feel inadequate.

In his book *The Fall of Public Man*, Richard Sennett talks of narcissism as self-absorption. It is an obsession, he says, with 'what this person, that event means to me'. This obsession with what events mean for the individual is so persistent that it frustrates any sense of fulfilment that might otherwise have come through that event. In being obsessed with self-gratification the narcissist is constantly denied fulfilment.

> Narcissism thus has the double quality of being a voracious absorbtion in self-needs and the block to their fulfilment.[4]

Narcissists are always searching for more meaning for themselves. In relationships with others they want to feel 'more' or talk about the relationship becoming 'more meaningful'. At each point they never seem to feel enough.

In a study of several hundred college-age young people in the late 60s and early 70s, psychoanalyst Herbert Hendin commented,

> This culture is marked by a self-interest and ego-centrism that increasingly reduce all relations to the question: What am I getting out of it? . . . Society's fascination with self-aggrandizement makes many young people judge all relationships in terms of winning and losing points. For both sexes in this society, caring deeply for anyone is becoming synonymous with losing. Men seem to want to give women less and less, while women increasingly see demands men make as inherently demeaning and regard raising a child as only an unrelieved chore with no objective rewards. The scale

> of value against which both sexes tend to measure everything is solitary gratification.[5]

Living for me, now

In his book *The Culture of Narcissus*, Christopher Lasch points out that this disorder has grown against the background of a society which focuses on therapy rather than on religion.

> The contemporary climate is therapeutic not religious. People today hunger not for personal salvation, let alone for the restoration of an earlier golden age, but for the feeling, the momentary illusion of personal well-being, health and psychic security.[6]

Modern men and women live for the moment. We who live in the modern world are little concerned with our predecessors and have a feeble idea of our place in history. Nor do we plan for the future, partly because of the pace of change in a technological society which defies prediction, and partly because modernity is deeply pessimistic about its own future.

> What has waned, perhaps, is the sense of living in a world that existed before oneself and will outlast oneself.[7]

The cult of the expert

In the public domain of ideas the problems have become so enormous that amateur involvement has diminished. We are in the age of the expert and we are happy to leave the solution of the world problems to them. At first sight what has happened is that individuals have retreated into a private realm which they can control. Behind their front door they can be relaxed and can find the personal fulfilment which is denied them elsewhere.

The problem is that although there has been a mass move away from the public domain into the private realm this too has become an unbearable isolation and not a place of fulfilment. Genuine privacy is simply not possible in modern society as even in our homes we are no longer always in control. In so many areas of our 'private' life – even in what we think, dream and lust after – we are no longer the experts.

> Having surrendered most of his technical skills to the corporation, he can no longer provide for his material needs. As the family loses not only its productive function but many of its reproductive functions as well, men and women no longer manage even to raise their children without the help of certified experts. The atrophy of older traditions of self-help has eroded everyday competence, in one area after another, and has made the individual dependent on the state, the corporation, and other bureaucracies.[8]

Here is a major cause of the insecurity of individuals in the modern world. Even when they are in their own homes, where they can 'be themselves', they are dependent on others. Even the expression of sexuality has become dependent on technique which has to be learnt from experts through manuals. The anxious mother is so insecure that when her baby cries she instinctively reaches for the child-care manual to tell her what to do. People approach marriage and parenthood as if they were mechanics trying to pass an exam in car repair.

This stripping away of dignity from people leaves them with a 'minimal self' and a sense of psychological nakedness. They feel that 'there must be more to life than this' and this leads to a frantic search for self-fulfilment. Sociologist Christopher Lasch talks of 'an anguished sense of failure, which gives added urgency for the quest for spiritual panaceas'.

This minimal self is expressed in the language of survival. People think they are lucky if they 'survive the week', and many people live from one holiday to another, seeing the work in between as merely a means of raising the money so that they can enjoy themselves on their next holiday. People no longer dream of tackling difficulties and overcoming them but merely of surviving them. Many of the disaster movies in our cinemas, and the talk of global environmental catastrophe, reinforce this feeling of impending disaster and the absence of any guaranteed future.

Escaping from this morbid scenario, individuals are driven inwards to find new resources to aid them to live. For this reason hundreds of different self-help and self-awareness philosophies have mushroomed over the last fifty years. These philosophies convince the individual that without giving up their obsession with themselves, help exists in the form of cosmic powers, yoga, health food, self-actualization, transactional analysis and many other ideas by which they can derive some comfort and consolation in a world in which God has been put to death and replaced by the quest for self.

> The ideology of personal growth, superficially optimistic, radiates a profound despair and resignation. It is the faith of those without faith.[9]

The causes of narcissism

What has caused this change in our social personality? Economic, philosophical and social factors have all contributed to its revolution.

1. Economic factors

The first cause, the *economic*, is attributed to the rise of capitalism. Erich Fromm has written a critique of capitalism which calls attention not to the economic injustice it creates but to the way in which it deprives the individual of unconditional love. He comments, 'The only satisfactory answer to the problem of human existence is love.' Capitalism produces psychological deprivation in that it teaches that people should get only what they deserve. At the heart of capitalism the market is a picture of people trading goods of equal value. But what people need is grace and unconditional acceptance.

Capitalism also encourages self-interest, which can quickly become self-gratification. This reduces love to manipulation of others for one's own ends. Even giving to charity, which appears to be altruistic, may turn out to have been done to increase self-esteem. Real love, however, does not focus on the self but on others. Love is therefore at odds with self-seeking.

Capitalism also offers personal consumption as an end in itself. Advertising projects fantasies for us which are associated with products which we are then encouraged to buy. Life is reduced to a process of production and consumption which, as we have seen in the previous chapter, is a form of idolatry.

Under this industrial capitalism individuals cannot flourish but are constantly reduced to the status of consumers of goods who deserve nothing more than equal value for what they can produce. Any act of grace in the form of unearned welfare is seen as an aberration and a dilution of pure capitalism.

It is ironic that the growth of capitalism owed its success to the egoist or the 'rugged individualist'. The dream was of the survival of the fittest. Those who built empires and who conquered all they surveyed were the architects of industrial life. But the complexity and increased bureaucracy of the modern world have so encroached on the individual that far from encouraging 'rugged individualism' it has given rise to dependency and to narcissism. Where the self reigned supreme the system has taken over and we have become servants and not masters of that system. Those who still dominate the skyline through the skyscrapers erected in their honour, are known as self-made people who owe nothing to anybody. Today they stand out as monuments to privilege and egoism, admired, despised and envied by those who live in the system that they have created.

2. Philosophical factors

Although the rise of capitalism is undoubtedly a contributing factor to the development of narcissism, a second factor is the rise of existentialism. This is a reaction against the scientific rationalism of the last century which stated that all events in the universe were fully explained and determined by the application of scientific principles. All that we feel and all that we are is reduced to the chance collision and interaction of atoms and molecules.

Existentialism (as expounded by Jean-Paul Sartre and Albert Camus, among others) pointed out that such a deterministic and fatalistic system excluded any meaning for human life. Chance reigned supreme and some scientists were honest enough to admit that behind the universe there was only a cosmic pair of dice. Sartre taught that by an act of choice an irrational meaning could still be found for life. Although there was no meaning for humanity as a whole, no divine plan being worked out through history, it was still possible for individuals to find something which gave their own lives meaning. For some it would continue to be religion, for others sex, for others sport or food or fashion. Whatever we chose was up to us as long as it made life bearable.

Existentialism is essentially a philosophy of isolation. We are thrown back on those things which give us hope and can never be sure that our personal choices are shared by those we love. The only tool the individual possesses with which to interpret the world, is his or her 'self'. It is the awareness of the fact of one's own existence, the 'I am' which is the only certainty. Death provides a real threat for this philosophy and leads to the presence of anxiety. The pressure on individuals is to develop themselves by a course of their own choosing so that their potential in life is fully realized. Failure to reach one's potential causes guilt; it is the ultimate waste of resources.

Vitz comments on existential narcissism,

> Intimate personal relationships become extremely dangerous. If you show weakness, such as a need for love, you get slaughtered; if you withdraw to a machine-like, emotion-free competence and develop complete identification with your career you are isolated and are starved of intimacy and love. Perhaps there is some relief in temporarily losing the self in sexual or other sensations and afterwards counting each new experience as a score for the self, but a lonely deathlike living is inescapable. This painful double-bind leaves love of the self as the diabolically 'safe' alternative.[10]

3. Social factors

The disintegration of society to which we have already referred gives rise to a family of factors which throw individuals back on those personal resources which themselves have been invaded by bureaucracy and the cult of the expert. The first important facet of this is the replacement of a culture based on religion by a culture based on therapy (as we have already mentioned).

We shall have much to say about the influence of the welfare state on the individual in chapter five but it is important here to note that the philosophy of welfare liberalism has sometimes been abused to such an extent that the individual is no longer treated as a responsible citizen but as a victim of social circumstances. It gives rise to a new administrative elite of bureaucrats on whom the underclass are dependent for benefits.

Poverty is an indignity in any age. But under modernity it means not only physical poverty but also a lack of community and of participation in decision-making. The elite who hand out benefits (thereby depriving people of a measure of individual responsibility) also create a culture for themselves. In it they have few responsibilities towards those who are less well off, but can entertain their fantasies undisturbed knowing that 'the poor are taken care of'.

As welfare has expanded the citizen has been reduced to a consumer of professional expertise. Even parents often feel helpless.

> Parents have little authority over those with whom they share the task of raising their children; they deal with

> those others from a position of inferiority or helplessness.[11]

The absence of the extended family exacerbates the sense of parental isolation and dependence. When grandparents lived with their children and grandchildren there was always the possibility of handing on wisdom in historical continuity. With the demise of the extended family wisdom has been replaced by the cult of the expert.

There is also an inappropriate romanticism about the nuclear family. The break-down of our common life has led to increasingly high expectations of one another. These expectations are focused on family life as if we could be 'all in all' to one another. Psychoanalysts tell us we crave intimacy but are fearful of disclosing our own vulnerabilities to others. We have unreasonable expectations of our partners because we are trying to derive that personal satisfaction from them which could be provided only by a complex of communal relationships.

These factors are compounded by a lack of faith in those who guide the public realm. In most major democracies voting levels are falling and there is a cynicism about the ability of politicians to rule over us. Along with our pessimism about the future, it hastens our retreat into the private sphere.

Os Guinness comments,

> . . .the private sphere is distinctively over-sold. It has become the sphere of spending rather than earning and of personal fulfilment rather than public obligation. Naturally then, when conspicuous consumption grafts spending into identity and fulfilment, appetites become insatiable and expectations unrealistic. In short, privatised man is not only an anxious Atlas, but a spoilt Narcissus. He wants more and he wants it now. After all, to others at least, he is what he consumes. And so is she.[12]

It may be helpful to show several areas of life which have been affected by narcissism.

1. Politics

Politics has been changed a great deal by the advent of narcissism. Although policies are still discussed, the image of the political leader is all important. (This is most obviously true in America.) In a culture that seldom asks, 'What am I doing?' but more often, 'What am I feeling?' or even, 'How am I relating?', how we feel about the 'image' of a political leader is now as important as the issues themselves.

In the 1987 British general election one of the key 'issues' was the way in which the leader of the Labour Party, Neil Kinnock, came over as a much stronger leader than had previously been envisaged. No political party can afford to have a leader who performs badly for the media.

In the 1988 American Presidential election the fight between Bush and Dukakis was in the end about the public image of the two men. George Bush who started with a weak image had a very strong team of public-relations experts who trained him to present himself differently until by the end of the campaign pithy sayings rolled easily from his lips in time for the evening television news. He appeared presidential and was accordingly voted in as president.

One other element in narcissistic politics is that it is increasingly assumed that the voter will vote in his own interests rather than using his vote altruistically on behalf of others. Politics now revolves around the self more than ever before. The big question every voter asks is, 'What is this party going to do for *me*?' People find it difficult to sustain an interest in those things which do not have some bearing on them personally.

Even with the issue of AIDS, studies show that young heterosexuals are not willing to change their sexual lifestyle unless they feel that their own life is threatened. The fact that they may infect somebody or even kill them by living promiscuously does not seem to concern them. The motto of the narcissist is 'Look out for Number One.'

2. Parenting

This is not an essay on psychoanalysis but it is important to note briefly that narcissism is a personality disorder. The three contributory factors (economic, philosophical and social) outlined above are important but it is thought that the formation of a narcissistic personality is dependent on how we bring up our children, especially in their earliest years.

There are two schools of thought among the experts. The first points to emotional deprivation in the early years as the cradle of narcissism. Children who have not had the love and security they needed in their early years are constantly seeking infancy.

The second school points to precisely the opposite – over-indulgent parenting. Children, it is argued, need to have constraints placed on them so that they can learn that people (including themselves) are not perfect. The job of the parent is to foster this healthy independence. Over-indulgent parents, in this view, only foster an obsession with the self. The child is not loved for himself, with all his obvious faults, but only for doing things which his parents praise.

It is probable that both permissive parenting and neglectful parenting may contribute in different ways to the development of a narcissistic personality. As the character develops the distortion grows.[13]

Narcissism produces a sense of dependency. The inadequacy which people already feel is heightened by the cult of the expert. Things which in earlier generations were done intuitively are now the preserve of the expert and in the area of parenting people turn to the manuals of child-care in order to get advice. With particular reference to the USA, Geoffrey Gorer says:

> The American mother depends so heavily on experts that she can never have the easy almost unconscious self-assurance of the mother of more patterned societies whose ways she knows unquestionably to be right.[14]

Another commentator suggests that

> The immature narcissistic American mother is so barren of spontaneous manifestations of maternal feelings, that she redoubles her dependence on outside advice. She studies diligently all the new methods of upbringing and reads treatises about mental hygiene. She acts not on her own feelings or judgment but on the picture she has of what a 'good mother' should be.[15]

3. Sexual intercourse

We have depersonalized sexual relationships. This is partly due to the fact that sexuality has, until recently, been expressed from the man's perspective. It has focused on the techniques of sexual intercourse rather than on fostering intimacy. We have reached the stage where sexual intercourse may actually be an avoidance tactic for some people who do not wish to be intimate. True intimacy admits vulnerability and is dependent on mutual self-disclosure. But sexual intercourse can take place according to certain objective criteria, the most important being the orgasm.

Many people whose bodies are not 'the right shape' or who do not have the right feelings and sensations in the right order are made to feel hopelessly inadequate. Sexual intercourse can, for them, be like putting on an agonizing performance where one is not sure of one's lines nor of whether the other participant is enjoying the show. When they have 'made love' they may even feel that they are being compared to their partner's previous lovers or merely to some stereotype.

No-one seems to be seriously questioning the popular assumption that sex is mainly for pleasure. But a lot of anxious people are not sure whether they are maximizing the pleasure for their partners or, indeed, for themselves. Because of this an area in human relationships which should be playful, non-threatening and affirming can become a battle-ground.

Anxiety in our sexual lives is a very important indication of the presence of narcissism. Rather than being secure in oneself, the need to be affirmed is paramount. One would have thought that in sexual intercourse a certain playful detachment is needed. 'Don't take yourself too seriously' might be good advice. But the thing one notices about people for whom sex is really important is how *serious* they are about it! Some have grown so narcissistic that they can no longer smile about it. Listen to some advice from Andy Warhol:

> The best love is the 'not to think about it love'. Some people can have sex and really let their minds go blank and fill up with the sex; other people can never let their minds go blank and fill up with the sex. So while they're having the sex they're thinking, 'Can this really be me?' 'Am I really doing this?' 'This is very strange. Five minutes ago I wasn't doing this, in a little while I won't be doing it. What would mummy say?' 'How did people ever think of doing this?' So the first type of person is better off. The other type has to find something else to relax with and get lost in.[16]

In a competitive and materialistic society, in which people, seeking affirmation, retreat into their inner selves, there is a yearning for intimacy. What people have found, however, is genital sexuality. Outside the context of intimacy they are not finding it particularly satisfying (as the divorce rate and the high turnover of relationships testify).

4. Spirituality

The fourth area where people look for a security which they do not find in themselves is spirituality. The proliferation of cults and the popularity of astrology all indicate that people want to be told that their life has meaning.

Sadly this is also true within the church. Many of the ways in which the world presents its narcissism also find some kind of expression in the church. In his lectures on 'The Cult of Narcissus', Roy Clements says:

> Is the world body-conscious? Well, then, the ladies will put on their leotards on Sunday afternoon perhaps and do 'aerobic praise'. Is the world obsessed with celebrity? . . . then the pastor will be presented as a celebrity. The very clothes he wears . . . will strike you immediately. This man is a personality! Is the world obsessed with yoga and mysticism? Then the church will offer ecstatic experiences of its own to the insecure who want to 'find themselves' in experiences with a Christian label.[17]

People do of course experience God in many different ways, some of them intense and very moving. But it is the craving for God to reveal himself in such experiences, and the accompanying feeling that God has somehow let us down when a meeting or prayer time is flat or boring, which are important to note. Roy Clements continues.

> Is our world obsessed with fitness and looking good; with the image of success? Then we will have wealth and prosperity doctrines in the church. Is the world obsessed with self? Then the church will subtly replace social responsibility with privatised piety; the kingdom of God with personal salvation; the prayer that begins 'our father' with a prayer that begins 'my father'; the agape of interpersonal fellowship with the eros of egotistical experience.[18]

Rather than constantly focusing on the self the Christian is self-forgetful and taken up with God. This emphasis runs counter to much of the modern-day emphasis on self-realization which is present in our therapeutic culture. Preaching on humility, repentance, forgiveness and judgment all run counter to the emphasis on achieving the potential of the self. Such lessons are hard for us to hear and even harder to understand.

For the moment we shall leave the problems raised by narcissism without any kind of solution. But we shall return to it when we consider worship and the security that we can find in God himself.

Before we leave the theme of the idolatry of the self it is important to form a bridge between this chapter and the next. In considering economics we shall be talking a great deal about self-interest. Capitalists and those Christians who defend capitalism still claim that if we all act in our own self-interest then all will work out for the common good. The most important conclusion which we can take from this chapter is that the way in which we view ourselves has changed decisively. *Where self-interest has become self-gratification it is no longer the case that 'market alternatives' will necessarily work out for the common good.* Could it be that capitalism has fundamentally changed in the context of the fragmented and secularized modern world? It is to this that we now turn.

CHAPTER FOUR

THE TYRANNY OF ECONOMICS

The ideas of economists and political philosophers both when they are right and when they are wrong, are more powerful than is commonly understood. Indeed the world is ruled by little else. Practical men who believe themselves to be exempt from any intellectual influences are usually the slave of some defunct economist. Madmen in authority who hear voices in the air are distilling their frenzy from some academic scribbler of a few years back. I am sure that the power of vested interests is vastly exaggerated compared with the gradual encroachment of ideas.

J. M. KEYNES

When I was at university I went to a party where two women students who were, like me, studying economics, said that they were hairdressers. When questioned afterwards they claimed that men were so insecure that they were threatened by 'brainy' women (a slight generalization perhaps). Even if this were not true, they said, the reputation of economists was so appalling that it was better to stick to being a hairdresser at parties. Now what hairdressers will think of this I do not know. They must balance the scarcely veiled insult to their intelligence with the obvious compliment to their 'social graces'.

Economists, whether male or female, seem to lose out all round (at least at parties!). To use the words of broadcaster John Pilger, spoken in another context, 'When they speak, silence falls round them like a moat.' Perhaps the problem is that they have been cast as the high priests of modern society. They have offered the Devil's temptation to Christ in promising the world to modern men and women and have not delivered on their promise. They have shouted 'Wolf!' and the crisis has not come upon us; they have foreseen revival and we have continued much as before.

It is not that we do not care about what economists are saying. We care 'too much'. But we are afraid to show just how deeply entrenched we are as a materialistic society. It is the job of the next two chapters to show in what ways *the economic point of view* has contributed to both the rise and now the threatened demise of the West.

Economics is a point of view in itself; a way of seeing the world. Many ideologies use the word as a label for a world-view. It is not a neutral word. Choosing to describe something in economic terms may be to choose too much even before anything ideologically controversial has been said. In the same way, to describe something through the written word is a choice from among alternatives such as conversation or the visual arts, even before a particular language is chosen. The power of economics is its application to almost any area of life and this is not generally understood by the lay person. He or she thinks of economics as being restricted to the realms of financial newspapers read by sober-suited people on commuter trains.

Many people would be astonished and not a little annoyed to see prestigious books such as Gary Becker's *A Treatise on the Family*,[1] in which the process of marriage and divorce is looked at economically. It seems that 'economic affairs' are not the only ones which interest economists! When we argue about something in terms of economics we may already have assumed too much. We have decided that economic categories are the right ones to use. Sociologist Peter Berger has often commented that once we have described something in economic terms we are reduced to 'knee-jerk reactions'.

We may have been better off evaluating the problem from moral, religious or social perspectives. But will a prior commitment to the economic point of view allow us to do this? Economics is a way of looking at life which has brought enormous benefits to us as a society but we must beware of its many traps for the unwary. Those things which prove most destructive to us in the long term are seldom overtly evil. People still believe in the right and the good.

Whatever the most insidious evils of our day will turn out to have been, from the perspective of history, it may well be that at the time we thought that they were working for our good.

Just as narcissism is the distorted face of contemporary self-idolatry, so the 'economic point of view' represents the distorted outlook of our society. All is subject to a 'balance-sheet morality' which appears to be both logical and reasonable but under whose influence not only is our society losing its human dignity but also its commitment to human community.

Modern people are 'homeless', looking for a redemptive community which will offer them a homecoming. We divide into two groups: those who are nostalgic, seeking community in some 'golden age' in the past which we constantly attempt to recreate; and the 'progressives', who look forward to creating community in the future when either revolution or reform has done its job. Either way, the perpetual quest for human community and for a sense of belonging is at odds with the way in which advanced industrialized societies are organized as economic systems.

The rise of the market

Humanity's survival on this planet depends on our ability to extract resources from the finite environment to feed, clothe and to nurture ourselves. Only a few ways have been found to organize society so that this can be done successfully. Most commonly it has been achieved by tradition, handing down tasks from generation to generation. It is still the case in India that some occupations are determined by caste. Another way is authoritarian rule. Whether it is the pharaohs or the politburo cracking the whip, this type of society is based on command. Neither of these societies has needed economists, for they function in a perfectly logical and foreseeable way.

But at the heart of the market system was a puzzle which needed to be explained. The evolution of markets for goods and services went hand in hand with the development of the explanation of how they operated. One reason for the late development of the market mechanism was the way in which medieval society used the building blocks of the market system; land, labour and capital. Land in medieval society was not freely saleable or rentable. It belonged to the lord of the manor – it was the basis of his power. Neither was labour for sale, for the peasant was tied to his lord and could not offer his labour for sale in the market-place. Nor did people take risks with capital, to invest it in projects. Safety was the rule.

Usury, the charge of interest on loans, was strictly banned by the dominant Roman Catholic Church and therefore the development of the market system took some time, starting as far back as the thirteenth century and not completed until the nineteenth.

To enable the market system to develop, Protestantism had to sire and encourage commercialism. Inventions such as the engine revolutionized industry. The infrastructure of roads and communication networks had to be built and the merchant class had to be free to make money, thus grasping power from the nobility. Previously this was seen as sin, but hard work, with its rewards, was now seen as a virtue. Efficiency started to enter into the exchange of goods and money. This system needed a philosophy. It needed people to explain and to judge it.

The most far-reaching of such men was Adam Smith, Rector of Glasgow University, who in 1776 wrote a literally world-changing book entitled *The Wealth of Nations*. This book explained his theory of economics and markets:

> It is not from the benevolence of the butcher, the brewer or the baker that we expect our dinner, but from regard to their own interest. We address ourselves, not to their humanity, but to their self-love, and never talk to them of our own necessities but of their advantages.[2]

Smith's view of the world was not based on 'cut-throat' competition but on a view of competition leading to social harmony.

> Every individual is continually exerting himself to find the most advantageous employment for whatever capital he can command. It is his own advantage, indeed, and not that of society, which he has in view. But the study of his own advantage naturally, or rather necessarily leads him to prefer that employment which is most advantageous to society. In this case, as in many other cases, he is led by an invisible hand to promote an end which was no part of his intention. I have never known much good done by those who affected to trade for the public good.[3]

Simply put, Smith's basic insight is that individuals who seek their own self-interest when they sell or buy in the market-place would find that if everybody else did the same, social harmony would result. As Robert Heilbronner has put it,

> In economics it is the lure of gain, not the pull of tradition or the whip of authority, which steers each man to his task.

He goes on,

> . . . for the market is not just a means of exchanging goods; it is a mechanism for sustaining and maintaining an entire society.[4]

It is important to put this in the context of Smith's earlier work, *The Theory of Moral Sentiments*. There he stated that the market operated within a framework of justice in which 'Natural Justice' sprang from each person's sympathy with the feeling of others.

> Justice was entirely necessary because otherwise flaws in the unregulated order would manifest themselves. There were certain conflicts of interest if each person's self-interest was not regulated by Justice, for competition could not always be relied on to optimize. Thus there was a conflict of interest between masters and workmen over the level of wages and a tendency for conflict to arise if the masters colluded to depress wages.[5]

Smith himself recognized the need to restrain market forces by the application of principles of justice. These principles were rooted in people's regard for one another socially, even if self-interest continued to be the driving force economically. But in our day this social restraint is breaking down, and the 'economic point of view' has come to dominate the modern world. This kind of thinking is defended by Nobel Prize-winning economist Friedrich Hayek when he says,

> Economic activity provides the material means for all our ends. At the same time, most of our individual efforts are directed to providing means for the ends of others in order that they, in turn, may provide us with the means for our ends. It is only because we are free in the choice of our means that we are also free in the choice of our ends. Economic freedom is thus an indispensable condition of all other freedoms, and free enterprise both a necessary condition and a consequence of personal freedom.[6]

Freedom mediated through markets, according to Hayek, is the basis of all our freedoms. We can dream dreams and seek to put them into practice only because we are free economically. Without economics we are in bondage. Such a radical philosophy, and the new society which represented it, would not have been possible were it not for that fundamental change of world-view which we have already referred to as the 'Enlightenment'.

A study of the Enlightenment, the seedbed in which economics grew up, is very necessary to a Christian understanding of economics. Adam Smith and David Hume were both leading figures in the Scottish Enlightenment. Much of the culture of our modern world dates from this period. Out of this furnace of change came capitalism, or what Robert Nozick has called 'commercial transactions between consenting adults'.

The emphasis was that 'free commercial transactions should not merely take place but should be permitted to shape civilisation as a whole'. As Irving Kristol has commented, no other society or civilization had ever said this before. Here is the difference between the presence of capitalism as a system and the presence of mere commercial activity in any society.[7] Most cultures placed other values above economics but in the new era economic values came to the fore.

For this reason capitalism could be defined as 'that system in which individuals who have the means at their disposal to exercise choice, are free to make decisions in their own self-interest about commercial transactions, which shape the values of the entire culture'.

This definition does not mention the behaviour of government or of trans-national corporations which may either enhance or destroy the freedom of individuals to make such decisions themselves. But the dominance of commercial decision making over other values is an inescapable part of economic life.

The consequences of economics

Concepts such as self-interest are fundamental to modern economics. How has it shaped our society? The Enlightenment emphasized the pursuit of private well-being and Smith legitimized self-interest by saying that only people who acted out of their self-interest would contribute to the public good.

But the fact that the market system distributes its benefits so unequally shows that something is wrong. In relying on self-interest the market system has legitimized one of the most dangerous human motives.

Of course, one strength of capitalism from a biblical point of view is that it does recognize that the system has to harness the drives of fallen people. A policy which depended on altruism may sound ideal but would never work in practice.

> In a large society, even if people were uncommonly well disposed to each other, how could they *know* what other's wants were? In fact altruism is only conceivable in very small communities where there is broad agreement about ends and purposes.[8]

The great paradox of market capitalism is that the unintentional consequences of our self-interest are said to be good for the community as a whole.

Professor Brian Griffiths, a Christian economist, states in his book, *The Creation of Wealth*, that it is possible to legitimize self-interest:

> Self-interest is a characteristic of the highest as well as the lowest kind of human behaviour . . . Indeed, as Christians we can go further and argue that self-interest as a characteristic of human behaviour cannot be divorced from that self-respect of which our Lord spoke when he told us to love our neighbours as ourselves.[9]

But can it be this kind of self-interest which drives the stock markets and motivates industry? In any case, this attempt to rehabilitate self-interest does not seem to have done much for the business community itself, for Brian Griffiths goes on to admit,

> I believe that it is only through the renewal of business with a moral purpose that we shall ever be able to meet the challenges facing us. The business corporation is a community. It requires leadership and at present it is desperately in need of a renewed vision of what is possible in business life in terms of the ideals of service, stewardship, community and justice under God. The challenge for the Christian businessman today is how to translate the vision into reality.[10]

Professor Griffith's attempt to reinstate self-interest in a more acceptable guise depends on the distinction between self-interest and selfishness. But this reasoning blurs the distinction between self-preservation (an instinct to every human being) and self-gratification (a consequence of human fallenness). It takes no account of the fact that in a narcissistic society 'conspicuous consumption' is an indication of one's status in life. The compulsion to consume in order to authenticate one's own existence is a modern phenomenon which is far removed from 'that self-respect of which our Lord spoke'. Indeed the way in which self-interest is manifested in modern society means that all is focused on the self. Can a system which is dependent on such a distorted picture of the individual still work out for the good of the community as a whole? I think not.

In fact the form of self-interest which is traditionally meant to drive business life would be unacceptable if brought into the home! People are asked to conduct their business affairs according to one set of principles and their social life according to another, focused on personal altruism.

Consequently, we are forced into a kind of 'doublethink'. In the market-place a self-interested commercial morality is regarded as sufficient moral guide. In social life altruism and generosity are expected. But to what extent can altruism be proffered by people who spend much of their professional lives admiring cold (albeit honest) ruthlessness based on self-interest? If the behaviour of the market-place is not to spill over into everyday life and begin to destroy community, some set restraints must be found to show people that such behaviour is not acceptable in society. This is the real problem we face when the economic point of view is unleashed without restraint, building an aggressively commercial society. The very drives which are most admired in the market-place are those which are most destructive of social communities.

The late Fred Hirsch, analysed this problem in his book *The Social Limits to Growth*.[11] Hirsch stated that after a certain level of consumption, people began to buy 'positional goods', goods which confer a certain status or ranking in society. Owning a house in an elite area might well qualify as there are only a restricted number of such houses. Possessing certain art treasures or belonging to certain clubs is coveted because these things say something about a person. Self-interest begins to creep into society until friends wonder whether they are themselves 'positional goods'. After all, one must 'know the right people'.

When Adam Smith advocated the use of markets in *The Wealth of Nations*, he did so in the context of the ample religious and moral constraints on the market at the time. Such constraints ensured that self-interest was kept in its place. As one commentator has remarked of Smith's vision,

> (People) could safely be trusted to pursue their own self-interest without undue harm to the community not only because of the restrictions imposed by the law, but also because they were subject to built-in restraint derived from morals, religion, custom and education.[12]

But in the 1930s the great economist John Maynard Keynes speculated on the future in his essay 'The Economic Possibilities for our Grandchildren':

> We shall then once more value ends above means and prefer the good to the useful. But beware, the time for all this is not yet. For at least another 100 years we must pretend to ourselves and to everyone that fair is foul and foul is fair; for foul is useful and fair is not. Avarice and usury and precaution must be our gods for a little longer still, for only they can lead us out of the tunnel of economic necessity into daylight.[13]

Keynes saw that a system of justified self-interest called fair, foul and foul, fair. His problem was that if society's goal was to become rich then means were more important than ends, and the useful more important than the good. Mankind must be led by its darker side. It may be customary for people in the business world to operate in this way in their dealings with each other, but what if such judgments come to dominate society as a whole? What will happen when friendship is merely a means to an end, or the arts robbed of their aestheticism because they have become mere marketable *objets d'art*?

As economist Fritz Schumacher said in his book *Small is Beautiful*, economics destroys the sacred, for it gives everything a price and nothing can be sacred if it has a price.

Is this not our position as a society at the moment? Are we not reeling from the subjection of successive areas of life to economic criteria? Where the arts, education, and health care become dominated by the criterion of economic feasibility, have not means been elevated above ends and the good subjected to the useful?

The economic sphere has become dominant. Fritz Schumacher comments:

> In the current vocabulary of condemnation there are few words as final and conclusive as 'uneconomic'. If an activity has been branded as 'uneconomic', its right of existence is not merely questioned but fundamentally denied. Anything that is found to be an impediment to economic growth is a shameful thing, and if people cling to it they are thought of as either saboteurs or fools. Call a thing immoral or ugly, soul destroying or a degradation of man, a peril to the peace of the world or to the well-being of future generations, so long as you have not shown it to be 'uneconomic' you have not really questioned its right to exist, grow or prosper.[14]

In his book, *Christianity and the Social Order*, Archbishop William Temple talks of the relationship between economics and other paradigms.

> Religion may rightly censure the use of artistic talents to make money of men's baser tastes, but it cannot lay down laws about perspective or the use of a paint-brush. It may insist that scientific enquiry be prompted by a pure love of truth and not distorted (as in Nazi Germany) by political considerations. It may declare the proper relation of the economic to the other activities of men, but it cannot claim to know what will be the purely economic effect of particular proposals. It is however entitled to say that some economic gains ought not to be sought because of the injuries involved to interests higher than economic; and this principle of the subordination of the whole economic sphere is not generally accepted.[15]

He goes on to say,

> We all recognise that in fact the exploitation of the poor, especially of workhouse children, in the early days of power-factories was an abomination not to be excused by any economic advantage thereby secured; but we fail to recognise that such an admission in a particular instance carries with it the principle that economics are properly subject to non-economic criterion.[16]

So where the influence of religion is in decline there will be a direct impact on economic life. Truth, trust, freedom, equity, restraint and obligation are all seriously affected when God is no more.

Markets need morality

Yet markets do need morality in order to work well. Where the culture is dependent on markets, but secularization has robbed the culture of Christian morality, some other means must be found to preserve markets from self-destruction. For without such a framework markets will become grossly inefficient. The problem is that the very morality they need to be able to function properly, is the very thing they tend to destroy.

The problem is that Christian values cannot be introduced piecemeal in order to shore up capitalism. It is not possible to focus on individual responsibility, honesty and the mandate to create wealth while ignoring the insistence on justice for those who are poor and oppressed. Yet this is a fault on both sides of the political spectrum. If one must have Christian morality then one must have all of Christian morality.

Neither capitalism nor socialism, however, is endorsed by a biblical world-view. Partly because of this and partly because of the continued dominance of economic values themselves, another language has emerged. With all the hallmarks of being a moral framework, it has the virtue, from the economic point of view, of being infinitely manipulable by the market.

This is the new 'morality' of *need*. Meeting needs has become the new justification for economic behaviour. To state that something is a need carries with it a new moral imperative and a sense of urgency. If I say that I want a new car, that can be questioned easily. But if I say that I need a new car I am stating something which nowadays has the status of a fact and is not to be questioned.

This language is insidious in the way it pervades our market behaviour. To state that something is a need is to state only half the case. Whether a need is moral or not can be determined by the answers to two questions.

Firstly, what do we need it *for*? Hitler needed the gas chambers to exterminate the Jews. The reason for the need gives the moral background and enables us to form an opinion. But in market capitalism we are told by the advertisers and marketing people that we *need* their goods. We need them to build up our image. They are wants masquerading as needs. But this language of need can provide a new justification for capitalism. The market, we are now told, 'is meeting needs'. Yet it is the market which is also creating those needs. In the midst of this, contentment is discarded as a virtue. For discontent is the engine of progress and without progress capitalism would die.

Those who see through such a false morality must constantly ask 'What do we need this *for*?' But secondly, we must ask, 'How did such a need arise?' If the need is seen to be legitimate, surely we face the question whether this need should have been allowed to arise. The starving are hungry. They *need* to be fed. But how did we get into a situation in this world where we have starving people in the first place? Surely our goal is to prevent such appalling need occurring.

A culture which has rid itself of Christian morality and replaced it with such shallow manipulation is merely covering the face of its own self-gratification with a moral cosmetic.

Capitalism and privacy

In a narcissistic society such as our present Western capitalism, self-gratification can so affect community life that instead of affirming community values, it erodes them, replacing them with an individualistic quest for privacy. Whereas communities depend on a willingness to relate to people very different from ourselves, capitalism reinforces our desire to mix only with those who are most like ourselves and at our convenience.

This has been admitted by such an outspoken apologist for capitalism as Ayn Rand who says in her book, *The Fountainhead*,

> Civilization is the progress towards a society of privacy. The savage's whole existence is public. He is trapped within the prison of family, tribe and caste. But under capitalism man is free to choose whom he will associate with, to choose whom he will value and befriend.

As we noted in chapter three this amounts to nothing less than the commercialization of love and the demise of community.

The cult of privacy, encouraged as one of the rewards of the capitalist system, is fundamentally opposed to Christ's teaching about the kingdom of God. It leads people (using their 'freedom of choice') only to associate with those who are like themselves. Luke records Jesus as saying:

> 'If you love those who love you, what credit is that to you? Even "sinners" love those who love them. And if you do good to those who are good to you, what credit is that to you? Even "sinners" do that. And if you lend to those from whom you expect repayment, what credit is that to you? Even "sinners" lend to "sinners", expecting to be repaid in full. But love your enemies, do good to them, and lend to them without expecting to get anything back.'[18]

Jesus is saying that the love of God is most evident when it crosses boundaries. Inviting to our dinner parties people who will invite us back is not demonstrating the love of God. There is very little difference between Christians and non-Christians on that point. It is when we associate with people most unlike ourselves that the love of God is most evident. Again we are asked to take a risk in the name of Christ. We are back to our argument in a previous chapter about the 'domain of control'.

Our society militates against this and proclaims the right of all people who have control over their circumstances to choose their friends, as Ayn Rand comments. But let us not be deluded into thinking that this is a Christian 'blessing'; it is the very antithesis of the values of the kingdom of God.

When suburban churches develop the atmosphere of the golf club, and a social whirl replaces true engagement with the world in mission, then all that is happening is that people are transferring values from the business-entertainment culture to their church life without asking the right questions. This has even developed into a strategy for mission, when we are told that 'only like can evangelize like'. In other words it takes rich people to reach rich people for Christ. Of course this may sometimes turn out to be true but it is no strategy for mission.

The culture which surrounds the market brings in the idea that one gets the standard of living, and now even the friends, that one deserves. The market is concerned above all with efficiency, and to give people more than they deserve would not be efficient. But love means unconditional acceptance of people. Such altruism cannot thrive in an aggressively commercial society in which the source of all love has been put to death.

When the world turns from its obsession with the self and with the economic, does it see in the church that new life ethic for which it so obviously longs? Or does it see a bunch of people behaving in a self-interested way? Can it see that Christian love is greater than self-interest? Can it see a contentment, which, like the pearl of great price, it would sell all to obtain? To what extent are we, the church in the West, a source of hope? To what extent are we a source of disappointment?

The idolatry of the system

Capitalism is driven by the engine of progress, a concept which has become a good in itself. To attack progress is to appear as much a fool as to uphold the uneconomic. Yet we are now extremely aware of the costs of progress. Our environment is suffering from the demands we make on it and we are only slowly becoming aware that resources are finite.

If we are to develop a new vision for economic life then three sets of values must change.

The spiritual agenda

Firstly, *self-gratification* must be replaced by *contentment*. This is the new spiritual agenda. In an age which feels its own inadequacy keenly and is distracted from it only by its discontent, this is no mean feat. To strive for inner contentment is to go against the tide of our own culture.

The behavioural agenda

Secondly, we must replace *conspicuous consumption* with *simplicity*. This is the behavioural agenda. There is no point in trying to achieve it if there is no contentment, otherwise resentment will quickly result. We must live appropriately in the light of the environmental challenge and the needs of others. We must also recognize the addiction of consumption and seek to release ourselves from its hold over us.

The policy agenda

Thirdly, we must challenge *rapid growth in the name of progress* and opt for *sustainability*. This is the policy agenda. Self-gratification in its obsession with self does not think about tomorrow. Yet we cannot claim to love our children and leave them with an inheritance of appalling need and global crisis. As stewards of God's world we must nurture and sustain it. Yet we cannot do so without simplicity and contentment.

We have a choice: the discovery of a new life ethic or increased fragmentation of community and ultimate catastrophe in the generations to come.

The choice is frightening, because we have divorced the economic from the spiritual and have no means or motivation to start again. Only by marrying the idolatries of the self and the system together does it become clear that any solution must begin, not with a change of policy, but with a change of heart. If the church abandons the economic agenda in favour of a privatized faith and neglects the demonstration of the extraordinary love of God in favour of the ordinary, on what foundation will we build our future life together?

CHAPTER FIVE

FAREWELL TO WELFARE?

All animals are equal but some are more equal than others.

GEORGE ORWELL

How can a people be free that has not learned to be just?

COMTE SIEYES

A culture may often be judged by how it treats its poor. In modern Britain we have created a welfare system which forms part of the economic system. A close look at it may well reveal the extent to which contemporary idolatry has infiltrated our common life. Can people be 'cared for' by a system, or is that a contradiction in terms? Does the welfare state mediate the strength of our compassion, or the coldness of our rejection, to those who are dependent on it?

Certainly the debate on the welfare system has changed radically over the last decade. The influence of 'monetarism' and 'Thatcherism' has been pervasive. In response, British socialists are beginning to adapt their traditional debating stance of egalitarianism, for socialism as a means to 'freedom'. The 'red flag' has become the 'red rose'. This process of adaptation means that the way in which key words and concepts are used is changing. Beside words such as 'freedom', 'equality' and 'social justice', what are 'market alternatives'? What does being 'free to choose' entail for a couple struggling on benefits? Surely if free markets create poverty they also create injustice?

Such questions are not easy to answer but it is important that Christians address them as they attempt to assess the current demise of the welfare state. For the most commonly reached conclusion is that the welfare state is not achieving its goals. Yet with one or two notable exceptions, no-one seriously wants to do away with it.

This leaves us 'tinkering' with the machinery as if the fine tuning were all that needed adjusting, when in fact the engine might need to be rebuilt. No-one, it seems, can face the enormity of that task, or thinks that they can do it any better. This phenomenon alone needs to be explained.

Perhaps it is to do with the intransigence of the problems reflected in the welfare state. It is not an isolated island in society, but draws its life from the wider context. For the welfare state reflects much of what we have become in modern Britain, especially in the decline of community awareness and the subsequent rise of 'welfare rights'.

The individualism which is so prevalent in modern life finds its expression in J. S. Mill's saying that 'The only freedom which deserves the name, is that of pursuing our own good in our own way, so long as we do not attempt to deprive others of theirs, or impede their efforts to obtain it.' Such a definition views other people only as possible constraints on our own freedom. Competition rather than co-operation is seen as the norm.

The biblical picture of freedom and obligation is quite different. In modern liberal orthodoxy people accept constraints on their anti-social behaviour because they do not wish others to behave in the same way towards them. However, in Old Testament law there are not only civil restraints but laws which require individuals to act positively and helpfully towards their 'neighbour'. My neighbour, then, is not a restraint on my freedom but someone whom I am to love as I love myself. The Mosaic law does not so much free me *from* others as free me *for* others.[1]

Of principal importance is the community of God's people of which the individual is a member. The law constantly requires individuals in any situation to ask themselves how they should behave in order to represent the life of that community. In Old Testament Israel it was *interdependence* which was valued, rather than *independence* in the modern sense of *autonomy*.

The Old Testament has no abstract definition of freedom, it does not deal with hypotheses which are hopelessly abstracted from the very lives which God has created. It does deal with the loss of freedom arising from exploitation, and from social and economic inequalities.

The prophets were extremely concerned about the share which families had in the land, which was the source of wealth. The most common routes into slavery were through war and debt, and a family or clan became vulnerable to exploitation when they lost their hold on their land. The prophets denounced those who accumulated property, 'who join house to house and add field to field, until there is no more room, and you are made to dwell alone in the midst of the land'.[2] The distribution of the land by God preserved economic independence.

In Israel people were equal in that all had been slaves and all had been liberated from bondage by God. One of the reasons for the degree of enlightenment in the Mosaic law about slavery is that it was an inappropriate category for someone who was 'the Lord's slave'. Similarly the wisdom literature points out that God created both master and slave, as the creation narrative implies.[3] Equality before God, not inequality, was God's norm.

Although the creation narrative contains a mandate to create wealth it seems that this wealth is to be used in the interests of the community. After all, as the Bible repeatedly points out, 'the earth is the Lord's' and we are merely trustees. In the Mosaic law God points people back to their own liberation as a reason for caring for the poor and oppressed. They are to reflect to others what God has done for them. There is therefore a strong motivation to act in the interests of the community.[4]

In modern society we have a welfare state because we have failed at being such a welfare society. The motivation to act in the interests of the community is lacking and self-interest is applauded. We have designed a system to care for our poor and needy, and we are proud of the vision which inspired it. But as we shall see, the outworking of the vision is constantly under pressure from the distortions which come from the fallen nature of our world. These distortions are so deep that no political structure can remove them.

In his teaching on the kingdom of God, Jesus extends the Old Testament teaching on freedom to talk about slavery to sin and the possibility of liberation.[5] His life and teaching inspired the early church to turn power relationships into relationships of mutual submission, and the church itself became a community of mutual dependence, spiritually, socially and economically. The Christian thinker is called to a sober realism about the extent to which any reform (or for that matter revolution) means genuine change, because of the pervasiveness of sin. He or she is, however, called to hope, because of the possibility of redemption. As Stephen Mott has commented,

> Sin is not the self-harmonising enlightened and rational self-interest of capitalist and other liberal forms of thought. Nor are human beings controlled by communal

> and creative drives assumed in traditional socialist thought. Sin is a power which destroys and must be restrained . . . Reliance on voluntary programmes of social care and the voluntary spirit of the people in place of legally supported programmes, exists upon a questionable basis from the vantage point of this interpretation of Biblical thought.[6]

The death of consensus

Even the debilitating effects of the culture of welfare might be forgiven if the performance of the welfare state were outstanding. After all, we are looking at the welfare state in such detail precisely because it is the 'secular' attempt to deal with the problems of distributive justice in our society.

The concept of the welfare state grew up in the days of consensus politics where Right and Left agreed substantially on the programme of action. The optimism about the management of the economy which had originated in the insights of J. M. Keynes meant that the existence of a redistributive welfare state was not seen as a problem since it could be financed out of growth in the economy. The problems really started with the recession of the mid-1970s brought on by the oil shock of 1973. It was here that problems of provision became evident. The 1970s saw the development of high and rising levels of unemployment and inflation together, and this could not be explained within the Keynesian consensus.

The year 1979 saw the election of a government which looked to the New Right and which saw the uncertainties in the market, caused by high and rising rates of inflation, as the main threat to society. The remedy of cutting public expenditure and the money supply, was bound to deepen the recession, leading to greater demands on the welfare system at the very time when it was bearing its share of the cuts.

Not only did the welfare system have to bear its share of the cuts but it came under withering attack from the 'New Right' which had been developing offstage for the previous thirty years, biding its time. This radical libertarian or classical liberal (not Liberal) view of the welfare state is quite different historically from the Conservative (Tory) perspective. Roger Scruton says of the latter in his book *The Meaning of Conservatism*,

> It is clear then what the conservative view of the welfare

> state must be. The English Conservative will not – like his American counterpart – regard it as an abomination, neither will he seek to extend it beyond the point which ordinary humanity requires. He will be reluctant to see the state make weaklings or dependents of its citizens, and yet at the same time he will not cancel what has become a hereditary right.[7]

The remnants of the consensus approach are most evident in the thinking of such politicians such as Norman St John Stevas and the late Earl of Stockton (formerly Harold Macmillan). His speech on 25 January 1985 argued strongly for a return to politics that would guarantee 'one nation', and he openly criticized Mrs Thatcher's policies. Here was a clash between traditional paternalistic Conservatism and the New Right, personified in the political commitment of a former and a present leader of the same party.

Mrs Thatcher's very different approach is evident in a speech she made in 1975:

> What lessons have we learned from the last thirty years? First, the pursuit of equality is a mirage. Far more desirable than the pursuit of equality is the pursuit of equality of opportunity. Opportunity means nothing unless it includes the right to be unequal – and the freedom to be different.[8]

It is the radical libertarians, on whose language and vision the Thatcher government has often drawn, that the Left have found it difficult to engage, let alone defeat, in intellectual debate. This is admitted by Bryan Gould, the Labour MP, in his book *Socialism and Freedom*. The Left has long assumed their opponents' acceptance of a trade-off between freedom and notions of justice and equality. This simplifies the debate, in that the only difference of opinion is exactly where on a continuum the trade-off should be made. In other words, How much freedom to create wealth and keep it should the individual give up so that, through taxation and redistribution, the poor may have more income and wealth? This is the model of the consensus era.

The problem with radical libertarians such as F. A. Hayek or Robert Nozick is that they reject the very notion of a trade-off. For them freedom is the overwhelming priority and also the means whereby all desirable social objectives can be realistically attained.

A left-wing defence against such a view has been slow in coming forward. Gould recognizes that

> The counter-attack would require an argument to the effect that there is no trade-off between liberty on the one hand and social justice, equality and efficiency on the other, . . . but that only by giving priority to the ideals of equality and justice is it possible to guarantee to everyone the maximum possible degree of individual liberty.[9]

The problem is that both Left and Right agree that the welfare state is a compromise which they are unhappy with for different reasons. Both sides dislike its bureaucracy, complexity, intrusiveness and failure to help those most in need. As Michael Harrington has remarked,

> There is the fundamental paradox of the welfare state; that it is not built for the desperate, but for those who are already capable of helping themselves.[10]

The Right see it as complex and bureaucratic, with too much discretion given to administrative officials and no accountability to the market. The Left see it as a vain attempt to graft a welfare sector on to a market economy. Julian Le Grand says of this,

> . . . a system was established that aimed to promote equality within a limited sphere. But by leaving basic economic inequality relatively untouched, it sowed the seeds of its own failure.[11]

Bryan Gould also states,

> The welfare state though valuable and important in itself, remains a palliative for dealing with the casualties of a system which necessarily produces major and self-reinforcing inequalities and injustices. The search for private profit remains the major motivation for economic activity.[12]

The provision of, for instance, the health service and state education, has benefited the middle classes more than the poor. On this both

Left and Right are agreed. Brian Abel-Smith commented as long ago as 1958 that

> . . . the major beneficiaries of the welfare state have been the middle classes, that the middle income groups get more from the state than the lower income groups, that taxation often hits the poor harder than the well to do, and in general that the middle classes receive good standards of welfare while the working people receive a spartan minimum.[13]

Indeed, whatever measure of equality is chosen to measure the performance of the welfare state, it does not deliver the dream in the way it was supposed to. Whether one is looking at housing, education, medical care or transport, the five definitions of equality used by economists show that we have not travelled far along the road to a more egalitarian society. This is true whether one is speaking of equality of public expenditure (which would spread expenditure on services equally among individuals), equality of final incomes (so that the incomes of the poor are brought into line with the rich), equality of use (so that the amounts of each service used by different individuals are the same), equality of cost (so that each individual faces the same cost per 'unit' of the service used) or equality of outcome (so that the individual's health or education, housing or conditions of mobility are improved). In some cases there might even have been greater equality had there been no public expenditure at all.[14]

What has happened is that the Left has made equality a means to an end rather than an end in itself. It is all too easy to measure the inequalies and to see that the welfare state has failed to deliver. Freedom is now the goal of both Right and Left. But whereas the Right see it in terms of minimal government intervention and the 'targeting of resources' leading to freedom of choice, the Left see freedom as giving people sufficient power to choose in terms of adequate resources. The difference between the old and the new debates seems to be sleight of hand.

As Roy Hattersley has said,

> As we evangelised for equality, we should have made clear that without it, for a majority of the population, the promise of liberty is a cruel hoax. Liberty is our aim. Equality is the way in which it can truly be achieved. It is time we made our ideological purposes clear.[15]

Markets, justice and power

The realization that the attempt to introduce egalitarianism through the welfare state has largely failed, has led right-wing libertarians to argue even more strongly for free markets as the only rational expression of justice. These arguments have been most cogently and powerfully expressed by Friedrich von Hayek, the Nobel Prize-winning economist and philosopher.

For him, the desire of those on the Left to cushion the poor from the problems of life is sadly misguided. Hayek points to the loss of dignity and the creation of dependency which we have already discussed. Freedom must include responsibility for our own actions and the absence of coercion, whether by the state or by other individuals. The problem for Christians is that the market creates wealth but it also creates poverty in relation to that wealth. As R. H. Tawney has said,

> . . . what thoughtful rich people call the problem of poverty, thoughtful poor people call, with equal justice, the problem of riches.[16]

One of the most draining and debilitating aspects of poverty in the UK or USA is that the poor person lives in a rich society where people are valued according to what they own. In a situation of absolute poverty it may be easier to retain dignity even in the midst of awful suffering. Where a whole people suffer, poverty does not point the finger of failure at the individual as poignantly and mercilessly as when poverty comes in the midst of affluence.

For Hayek, freedom is the absence of *intentional* coercion from another person. Injustice occurs only if the action is both personal and deliberate. As he often points out, the outcome of market transactions is the product of human action but not of human design. Those who trade in the market-place do not intend that their actions should create poverty for others. Moreover, poverty on this view is an incentive. Inequality is necessary since it stimulates people to create wealth.

Poverty on this view is not injustice but 'bad luck'. When strong winds devastated the south of England in 1988, several people suffered the loss or damage of their homes. Could they claim that this was unjust? No, because the wind was not responsible for what it did. In the same way, Hayek claims, one cannot blame the market for any damaging outcome of its operations. The free market is a game in which the winners are those who are simply better at the game or who have more luck. The fact that life has dealt some a severe blow does not give them the right to other people's money, as if the rich were responsible. To tax their wealth is to use state coercion and to violate their rights. Too high a tax ratio will kill incentive. Social justice, far from increasing freedom by reducing inequality, as in Gould's view, prevents people from achieving what they could achieve.

But justice should not be concerned only with the origin of poverty, and whether society can be held responsible for it. It should also be concerned about the way in which society responds to the existence of poverty.

Although people may not intend poverty to be exacerbated when they buy or sell on the market-place, this effect can be foreseen. There may be no point in accusing the wealthy and the powerful of intending to create poverty and misery, but we can at least say they could foresee that some people would feel (and be) poorer as a result of their getting richer. It is their failure to act on this foresight which constitutes an injustice. Dives ended up in torment not because he caused the poverty of Lazarus (we are not told that he did), but because he failed to alleviate it, thereby perpetuating it.

One other criticism of the political Right comes with the erosion of the principle of social insurance. At least when people paid their own way they received services in accordance with their payments. But when taxation takes over as the source of funding, several things happen. Firstly, the system becomes a vast administrative bureaucracy. Secondly, because of this, officials discriminate between clients on very subjective grounds. Thirdly, and paradoxically, there has been a tendency for central government to behave as if it had some objective criterion of need which it could apply to people.

So, given that both Right and Left are now talking about freedom, and given that both are critical of the past performance of the welfare state, what is it that people now have a right *to*? How are those rights to be expressed?[17] Is the language of human rights an appropriate language in this area or is that language covering up our failure as a human community? It is to these issues that we now turn.

Rights and responsibilities

It is here that the nub of the problem is reached, as is pointed out by Lesslie Newbigin in his Gore Lecture *The Welfare State – A*

Christian Perspective.[18] Newbigin points out that the welfare state sits rather uneasily on a market system designed around different principles. For the welfare system is centred on the concept of *need* whereas the market reflects *wants* (although, as we have seen, these wants are often dressed up as needs). Thus the fact that many in the population still lack basic commodities such as decent housing or nutritious food does not stop industry turning out more luxury items in response to wants. Moreover, the uneasy partnership of these two systems confuses the important issue of human rights, a problem which hits at the very heart of the welfare state.

The language of human rights has gained more than a foothold in political debate over the last twenty years. Some would say that it has gained a stranglehold, for if everything is a right then nothing is a right and more and more seems to fall into the rights category. This development indicates an increase in powerlessness, for as people feel powerless they attempt to label what they have lost as theirs 'by right' (*cf.* the current emphasis on the 'right to work'). But are rights determined by want or by need?

Libertarians, who stress the rights of the individual, state that whatever the individual wishes to do with his income and wealth should be of concern to nobody else and no-one else has a right to his property. They reject the idea that welfare is some kind of moral right, seeing it more as a matter for compassion, charity and largesse rather than for justice, and certainly not for extensive state political action. Those on the Left believe that our humanity places upon us an obligation or duty to care. Although such an obligation could conceivably be discharged voluntarily, it is not, and state coercion via the tax system (including wealth taxes and restrictions on the mobility of capital) must be used to bring about justice.

Lesslie Newbigin points out that both parties to the debate have their roots in the Enlightenment. Both sides claim to be defending human rights and human happiness. But who can decide what human happiness really is or what somebody else needs? Unfortunately the government has no omniscient planners. To state what another person needs is to claim a degree of knowledge and insight which does not exist. This means firstly that there can be no unique standard of *need* and secondly, that the government, which acts as though it has more information than the population and therefore is able to define what need is, is operating under a 'fatal conceit'.

The heart of the support for the market economy made by the Right is a belief in the autonomous nature of man. By stressing that, they wish to emphasize all that is good about individual responsibility and human dignity. But surely no biblical Christians can accept the autonomy of people as a basis for thought. The Bible tells us that the one thing which was not good in God's creation was that man was alone. It was man in community, humanity as male and female which was pronounced good. The Christian wishes to stress not independence but *interdependence*. The welfare state only becomes necessary because we have failed to be a welfare *society* in which we would voluntarily accept a natural obligation to care for one another.

Interdependence would have many consequences. Because we have accepted that individuals are autonomous, we have also accepted the demolition of the concept of 'charity'. As Newbigin points out, charity is an affront only to the would-be autonomous individual. In other cultures (he cites India), where interdependence is expressed towards the poor by charitable acts, there is no stigma, for there is no tradition of the autonomous individual. Caring for one another should be a privilege, the carrying out of which frees the individual from the need to claim rights.

In a society such as ours where people are retreating into themselves and the concept of interdependence is almost non-existent, the strain will be taken by the concept of human rights. But when the claim to rights is made by different interest groups, so that society becomes competitive rather than co-operative in the search for higher welfare levels, the ensuing battle can destroy the fabric of society.

If we cannot prevent such competition by defining 'need' objectively for the country as a whole, and if we cannot accept the autonomy of the individual and his or her wants as a basis for rights, what are we left with? For the debate over the welfare state will be unresolved as long as it is conducted as a search for alternative bases for rights, whether expressed in terms of 'wants' or 'needs'.

At the heart of the Christian insight about rights lies the fact that 'in the actual presence of God none of us can claim rights, not because God overrules us with his power but because he does not'. For,

> . . . If justice is taken out of its true context in the holy love of God as the law of human being and placed within the Enlightenment view of the human person as an autonomous individual, the result can only be disaster.[19]

The church needs to lead the way in visibly rehabilitating the concept of 'charity' or 'loving care', not as an option as some on the Right would have us believe, but as the motivation for the duties and responsibilities we have to one another, without detracting from the quest for greater justice in society. As we recognize that clinging to wealth in the name of rights has much to do with fear, and that interdependence is our natural state, should it not be possible to strip charity of its stigma?

I have been using the word 'justice' in its popular senses. The Right sees it as inextricably bound up with the absence of coercion on the individual who is free to do as he or she wishes. The Left sees it as bound up with the pursuit of economic equality. From these roots many different concepts can be drawn out. The work of Rawls, Nozick, Hayek and others all appeal in some way to these two traditions. But the biblical starting point for a definition of justice is quite different. Justice is rooted in the holy grace of God. Grace and justice are not separate from one another. By God's grace we can all belong to his family. We can all experience kinship or community because God has made it possible. From the biblical point of view *justice is doing what is required to make it possible for everybody to belong in the community.*[20] It is probable that the Jubilee of Leviticus 25:8 – 55 was never actually carried out, but the concept of justice enshrined in it is undoubtedly centred on the need to protect people's place in community and the health of the community itself. The focus of the biblical concept of justice is the person in community and encompasses both legal and socio-economic aspects often kept apart in secular discussion. In particular the biblical picture incorporates both the personal and the social in its holistic approach. We shall expand on this theme in later chapters.

The needs of strangers

Julian Le Grand states at the end of his study of the welfare state, 'To understand what people believe it is crucial to understand the way they behave; and to change the way they behave it is crucial to change what they believe.'[21] This echoes Erich Fromm in his book *To Have or To Be* in which he states that to change society it is necessary to change the human heart. As we have already commented there is an inextricable link between the personal, the social and the spiritual. If the creation of a welfare state starts with a grand vision of provision and then degenerates into a means of rejecting those it provides for, this is because people will it that way.

In a democratic society the state of the human heart can be plainly seen, reflected in the culture it gives birth to. No amount of talk about rights can make up for a lack of community or love. No system can give dignity to people.

This is one of the themes of Michael Ignatieff's book, *The Needs of Strangers*. [22] He comments that because we live in a welfare state the entitlements of others tie them to us albeit in an extremely tenuous way. As I queue behind an old age pensioner in the post office some minute portion of my income is transferred from my pocket to hers. Ignatieff comments, 'We are responsible for each other, but we are not responsible to each other.'[23]

> The political arguments between right and left over the future of the welfare state which rage over these old people's heads almost always takes their needs entirely for granted. Both sides assume that what they need is income, food, clothing, shelter and medical care, then debate whether they are entitled to these goods as a matter of right, and whether there are adequate resources to provide them if they are. What almost never gets asked is whether they might need something more than the means of mere survival.[24]

There is more to a person's self-respect than having his needs recognized as human rights. But to say that people have needs which are not easily defined in political terms is to imply that politics has a wider function which it is important for the community to recognize.

Ignatieff rejects the modish language of human rights as being incomplete in that it cannot include the need for virtues such as respect and love. We should create a language of human needs, he says, which can 'define what we are in terms of what we lack'. This is interesting because (as we have seen in chapter four) the language of human need as it is currently used expresses 'economism', which is materialistic in an even narrower sense than the language of human rights.

The difference between the language of needs as used by the advertising profession and as expressed by Michael Ignatieff is that the former is about *having* while the latter is about *being*. The language of economics cannot say anything about the needs of *people* because it views them only as bundles of consumer preferences. To the economic eye the self grows or dwindles as it accumulates or de-accumulates. The idea that a person rich in material terms may be poor in other senses including the spiritual and emotional is not accessible to economic reason. But the idea that people are similar enough to be able to talk about their needs in terms of what they lack as people, in order to heighten their sense of dignity and human self-respect, is quite different.

This has implications for the right-wing view that economic freedom (being free to choose) is the most fundamental value in life from which all other values are derived. I do not need to be loved in order to be free, but to be loved and to love. Nor do I need to be free (economically) in order to love.

> There does exist a set of words for these needs – love, respect, honour, dignity, solidarity with others. The problem is that their meanings have been worn out with casual over-use in politics. They have been cheapened, not only by easy rhetoric, but also by the easy assumption that if a society manages to meet the basic survival needs of its people, it also goes some way towards meeting these more intangible needs. Yet the relation between what we need in order to survive and what we need in order to flourish is more complicated than that.

It may well be that politicians are still talking about love and respect for the poor but that those who depend on the welfare state cannot discern how the rhetoric affects them. Ignatieff continues,

> Giving the aged poor their pension and providing them with medical care may be a necessary condition for their self-respect and their dignity, but it is not a sufficient condition. It is the manner of the giving that counts and the moral basis on which it is given: whether strangers at my door get their stories listened to by the social worker, whether the ambulance man takes care not to jostle them when they are taken down the steep stairs of their apartment building, whether a nurse sits with them in the hospital when they are frightened and alone. Respect and dignity are conferred by gestures such as these. *They are gestures too much a matter of human art to be made a consistent matter of administrative routine.*[25]

The problem is that human respect comes in two forms. As mediated through the welfare state it means that every individual has to be treated like every other individual. Our survival needs are the same. But respect also means that I treat each person as unique, giving deference to the character and situation of each person. The fact is that no system can treat people with individual respect. It is the virtue of the system that it processes people with great efficiency because it is able to fit them into certain administrative categories. Each story told with feeling becomes a series of holes on a computer tape. Having a story which is unique may mean that the system cannot cope and will refuse provision. Only where the rules apply will provision be made and only where real people fit the models of people in the system can lives be reduced to payments.

No system can deliver love. What people are looking for is to be drawn into a set of relationships. In a community people learn about each other's needs and how the uniqueness of the individual bears upon our common needs. This is why being dependent on the welfare system often feels like rejection. The person behind the grill at the benefit office wants no relationship with you. He will not put on his coat and invite you out for a drink to discuss your problems. You are a client.

People want intimacy with others and such intimacy depends on mutual self-disclosure. Two people must lower their defences enough to admit that they are vulnerable and have wants and needs to which even they only half admit. Such intimacy seems entirely inappropriate in a discussion of welfare since all the system can provide is a one-way, materialistic, impersonal dependence. Such is not the stuff of human flourishing!

Much of this book is about the necessity for Christian involvement in the public arena and the spirituality which complements such a move. Yet the need for such involvement in life is not only dictated by a biblical commission but by the limits of politics. It turns out that it is not enough to leave life to the politicians. Not only is the language they speak inadequate to circumscribe all of life but the political vision is too pragmatic to begin to satisfy the human need for the transcendent.

> There are other needs, besides love, which test the limits of what politics can possibly offer. We are the only species with needs that exceed our grasp, the only species to ask questions about the purposes of our existence which our reason is unable to answer. Contemporary politics is largely silent about this need for metaphysical consolation and explanation, but, next to love, it is one of our strongest promptings and one which is utterly

> unreconciled to the limitations of our ignorance. Is there a secular politics capable of satisfying this need for ultimate meaning?[26]

Materialism provides a paucity of political vision which stops far short of those attitudes and relationships which people need in order to flourish. In place of any such vision the promise of progress and the rationale of need create a private world in which we are free to enjoy being with people like ourselves while cutting ourselves off from 'the poor'. In such an atmosphere the language of human rights has come to give us 'our daily bread', but it is an atrophied and overworked language.

Such a society needs salvation, it needs a vision of God and of his transcendence. It also needs Christians who will realize that our involvement in society cannot be predicated on the philosophies of Left or Right. The Christian's quest for justice is rooted in the doctrine of God and it is the justice of God to which we now turn in order to start to build a response to our society's organized sterility.

CHAPTER SIX

JUST GOD

Because of God's own care for the poor, and because of their exploitation by the unscrupulous and their neglect by the church, they should now receive a 'positive' or 'reverse' discrimination. The church should concentrate its ministry where the need is greatest, to move from the centre out 'towards the periphery', to the 'sinned against', in other words to the poor and oppressed.

JOHN STOTT

If idolatry is the starting place and the correct context in which to consider the problems we are facing in the modern world, then the right starting place for any Christian response must be with the true God. Idolatry twists and distorts the truth about God and therefore about us and our society. It announces the death of God and leaves us to live with the consequences in ourselves and in our social and economic life. But if we root all that we are and all that we do in a right view of God, there will be far-reaching effects.

From the beginning we must be sure of one thing. Christians involved in society have only one starting place for their thinking and one foundation on which to build: the person of God himself. Those who are involved in politics are not or should not be involved because of a prior political commitment to the Left or Right. These are merely inadequate and imperfect tools. It is because the God we serve is a God of justice that we must have a passion for justice. It is because he does justice that we must get involved rather than being armchair commentators. It is because he has suffered in the cause of justice, that we must be ready to suffer in the service of others.

We are called to be imitators of God, he commands us to 'be holy even as I am holy'. This holiness is not only a negative separation from all that is evil but a positive demonstration of all that is good. We are not to be known only for what we stand against in this world but also for our likeness to God himself.

We have already commented on how we have the constant tendency to go through life setting our own standards by those of the rest of society. It is when we see what God considers to be the norm that we find how far we are from his standards. God, in revealing his holiness, shows us the ultimate standard by which all else is to be judged. He reveals his holiness in many ways but primarily in his 'righteousness and justice'. Isaiah tells us that '. . . the Lord Almighty will be exalted by his justice and the holy God will show himself holy by his righteousness'.

What do these two words, righteousness and justice, really mean? Many people today use the word 'righteous' only in the term 'self-righteous', describing people who put themselves forward as the standard of moral behaviour. In Hebrew the word usually translated 'righteous', *ṣaddîq*, means 'straight'. Psalm 23:3 tells us that the Lord 'guides us in paths of righteousness'; literally, straight paths. Similarly when the trader in the market-place is instructed to use 'honest scales and honest weights . . .' he is told to use 'righteous' equipment. In his book, *Living as the People of God*,[1] Christopher Wright comments that righteousness means 'something which is fixed and fully what it should be and so matches a norm'.[2]

Justice (*mišpaṭ*) is a dynamic word, a word of action. It describes what has to be done to a society to restore it to its norms. If business dealings are being conducted using false weights and measures, thus depriving people of food and exploiting them, then justice demands that the trader be punished and the false weights destroyed. If idolatry is widespread then a cleansing process must take place. If landowners are oppressing the poor, or lenders charging interest against the law, then this must be rectified. It is because the norms enshrined in the law reflect God's own character that they are a normative standard. They reveal his holiness and are therefore required of his people. If his people do not demonstrate them then they no longer reflect the character of God. As Stephen Mott has commented,

> Our justice corresponds to God's justice just as our grace corresponds to God's grace and our love to God's love.[3]

God loves justice. He declares in Isaiah 61:8 that 'I, the Lord, love justice.' The psalmist says, 'The Lord works righteousness and justice for all the oppressed' (Psalm 103:6). The next verse then applies this by saying that 'He made known his ways to Moses, his deeds to the people of Israel.'

What is the character of God's justice? Again the psalmist spells it out. God is the one who

> . . . upholds the cause of the oppressed
>   and gives food to the hungry.
> The Lord sets prisoners free,
>   the Lord gives sight to the blind,
> the Lord lifts up those who are bowed down,
>   the Lord loves the righteous.
> The Lord watches over the alien
>   and sustains the fatherless and the widow,
> but he frustrates the ways of the wicked.[4]

This justice is for all the people of the earth and not just God's people. There are not two standards of behaviour (*cf.* Jeremiah 9:24). This verse also points out that the person who claims to be wise and to know God will be someone who

> . . . understands and knows me,
>   that I am the Lord, who exercises kindness, justice
> and righteousness on earth, for in these I delight.

God's special concern is for those who cannot secure for themselves those things to which they have a right. God's justice is not merely retributive; he is not concerned only with punishment. God does not delight in that. God is concerned with distributive justice. Our fallenness has blighted the world which he made. Instead of all enjoying 'shalom' (wholeness or completeness as well as peace), many are oppressed and poor. This was not his intention and he cares for each person who has fallen foul of injustice.

In any society the strong and powerful secure all they need for themselves. But the poor and the needy do not. If God does not champion their cause, who will? If God's people do not act as his agents in that cause, how will his intentions be put into action? When God's people cease to reflect God's image, through apathy or idolatry, they not only cease to be a witness to the nature of God in the world; they also cease to carry out God's mission to the world. The test of a society is not whether the rich are secure in their wealth but whether the laws and practices of that society secure all that is needed for the poor. Do the economically powerless have enough? That is the question.

This does not mean that God does not love the rich and powerful. Christ died for the whole world. But there is a double offence in the fall. Our sinfulness is not only an offence against God the Redeemer. It is an offence against God the Creator. God created a world for everybody to enjoy. His desire was that all should enjoy the earth to the full. Now the squalor of poverty is an offence to God. As the writer of Proverbs puts it, 'He who mocks the poor shows contempt for their Maker.'[5]

As Nicholas Wolterstorff points out,[6] the good shepherd leaves the ninety-nine sheep in the fold because they are safe and goes after the one who is lost. Does this mean that he does not care about the ninety-nine? Not at all. But they are not his priority at that moment. Similarly, God suffers when his creatures suffer. His heart goes out to them. He desires that they should have the best. He took the trouble to make them and even if they are in rebellion against him he will still care for them. After all, if our hearts go out to those who are suffering from malnutrition; if anger burns in us at the torture of the innocent; if smug apathy over squalor sickens us, how does God feel? Do we not feel these things because we are made in his image.

God's justice is therefore an expression of his grace. He is not impartial and aloof like a high court judge. That is not an appropriate picture of justice in this context. If God is to be perfectly just in an imperfect world then he must constantly 'lift up' those who by no fault of their own have fallen by the way.

> What the secularist sees merely as good things coming his way, the believer sees as gifts from God. What the secularist sees merely as a stupendously intricate world, the believer sees as the glorious work of God. What the secularist sees merely as wrongdoing, the believer sees as sin. So too, what the secularist sees merely as justice, the believer sees as giving God joy. And what the secularist sees merely as injustice, the believer sees as making God suffer. For the believer, justice and injustice are sacramental realities. God loves the ninety and nine along with the one; but he suffers over the plight of that one.[7]

One of the most important facets of God's gracious justice is his 'positive action to create and preserve community'.[8] Where the fallen systems of this world tend to push the powerless to the margins of society, God is concerned to include them in community. In fact they are placed at its heart. God's gracious love towards the poor and oppressed means that justice is not restricted to the equal treatment of equals. God's love is directed equally to all, respects all and rejoices when people enjoy shalom in God's world. Because of this God's love is at the heart of the concept of human rights, which is the very root of justice.

God's concern for the weak needs to be set out carefully if misunderstandings are to be avoided. God does not turn a blind eye to the sins of the poor. God is especially concerned about the excluded because they are the objects of injustice which cause him to suffer. We may find it ironic that the prophets constantly see this expression of gracious justice as evidence of God's impartiality, in that it shows that he is not on the side of the rich and the powerful. Throughout history and no less in modern times, the rich and powerful are always eager to have God on their side, claiming that their wealth is evidence of his favour, when in fact it may be built on wickedness and exploitation, or constitute a call to accept material responsibilities for bringing about justice. Wealth is not neutral in a world in which God's priority is for the poor.

The children of Israel were to act justly towards others because God had acted justly towards them. Justice in this case means 'vindicated' or 'delivered'. The children of Israel were slaves in the land of Egypt and God graciously delivered them in an exodus which provided a picture of the redemption to come in Christ. Because they had received such a gracious deliverance, they were to act towards those who were in similar situations with the same heart as God showed towards them.

> He defends the cause of the fatherless and the widow, and loves the alien, giving him food and clothing. And you are to love those who are aliens, for you yourselves were aliens in Egypt.[9]

There were, therefore, two major motivations for Israel to act justly. Firstly, there was their own deliverance and subsequent equality together before God as his redeemed people. Secondly, they were aware that they were responsible to God for one another simply on the grounds of their common created humanity. As Job says,

> If I have denied justice to my
> menservants and maidservants
> when they had a grievance against me,
> what will I do when God confronts me?
> What will I answer when called to account?
> Did not he who made me in the womb make them?
> Did not the same one form us both
> within our mothers?[10]

It is important then that we distinguish between God's righteousness and justice in general providence and in redemption. Christopher Wright puts the distinction helpfully when he states,

> Every act of redemption is an act of righteousness, but not every act of righteousness is part of his redemptive purpose. What occurs within God's overall, providential ordering of human affairs, as sovereign Lord of the whole of creation, is wider than the scope of his redemptive activity at any one point in history. Therefore, when the oppressed are liberated, or certain wrongs righted, or justice executed, we should not regard any or every such event or process in and of itself as part of God's redemption. We should, however, certainly want to affirm such things as part of the providential will and ordering of God the Creator and righteous Judge of all men.[11]

Even though an act of justice might not be an act of redemption this does not mean that we should attach any less importance to doing justice. God the Redeemer and God the providential Creator are one God, not two. He is still the 'lover of justice'.

The message of the prophets concerning economic injustice therefore presupposes that Israel has departed from God because the people have neglected to do what God both revealed to them and required of them. In their social life the Israelites betrayed God and their own roots in his righteousness. Since God is the source of justice, knowing God is prior to doing justice. The prophets link Israel's tragic failure to 'do justice' to her failure to 'know God'.[12]

Rejection of God means that community life begins to crumble away because God is its guarantor. Israel knew, in those times when she was faithful to God, that both her responsibility to the poor and their rights were rooted in God's gracious justice. It was not some quality inherent in the poor person but in God himself which meant that the people of God were to do justice. It was God to whom they were accountable for their actions. When they ceased to perceive God as the initiator and sustainer of their social and economic life the bonds which bound them to one another began to slacken. They lost sight of their common equality before God. Consequently they slipped into idolatry which was invariably linked to oppression, greed and violence.

Stephen Mott points out that biblical justice is different from the more usual concepts of justice. In most secular views of justice a disruption of society is settled justly when society is brought back to the position before the disruption. If one's former position was one of disadvantage then such a view of justice will only restore one to that position.

> As they were not equal before, they will not receive equal shares in the benefits awarded in the redress. Marginal people remain marginal after justice is finished. Through the creative power of biblical justice, however, the individual's ability to contribute to the community is not merely preserved but actually created by justice.[13]

The Scriptures do not therefore allow us to tolerate a situation in which groups or individuals are excluded from participating in the life of the community. Each person must be strong enough to hold his or her own in relation to the other members of the society.

Israel was created as a nation by God in such a way that each family and clan had a portion of land which was the source of their wealth and therefore of their economic freedom. This basic equality was guaranteed by the operation of the Mosaic law and particularly the laws of Jubilee which stipulated that every fifty years all land had to be returned to its original owners. It was therefore not possible for Israel both to obey the law and to allow individuals to accumulate land. Even if a person had become a debtor to such an extent that he was forced by circumstances to sell his land it had to be returned to the family on the day of Jubilee. Not only did this happen but all slaves were set free and all debts cancelled. Each family therefore had an opportunity for a new start. Jubilee testifies to the fact that God had built into the law a fundamental equality not only between individuals but also between extended family groupings.

Similarly there was a ban on interest throughout Israel. Interest could not be charged to a fellow Israelite since they were equal before God and interest was perceived as a burden on the poor. It was possible to charge interest to other nations, for instance to the camel trains that passed through Israel. This would have prevented Israel from being exploited by other nations as a source of cheap loans and therefore bankrupting her economy.

Throughout the Old Testament law God's gracious justice for the poor is evident. Tithes were used to provide for the Levite, aliens, orphans and widows. If anyone required a pledge for a loan he was not to go into a house to fetch it but to stand respectfully outside, wait and have it brought to him. If the pledge consisted of a cloak then it was to be returned before sunset because it would be needed to keep the person warm at night. Wages were to be paid the same day they were earned. Farmers were to leave the boundaries of their fields when harvesting so that the poor could 'glean' the crops (as in the book of Ruth). Neither were they to strip their vineyards of fruit or pick their olive branches a second time. The poor were to share in the harvest celebrations. Every three years a tenth of the harvest was to be given to the poor. Every seven years land was to lie fallow and vineyards and olive groves were to go unharvested so that the poor could be fed. God promised that those who were faithful to this would have enough in the sixth year to last them for the seventh year as well.

Not only were justice and righteousness inculcated in the attitudes of God's people but they were enshrined in the very socio-economic structure of Israelite society. Not only was personal righteousness a hallmark of Israel but structural righteousness was evident as well. Israel as a society was a light to the nations. Indeed the society, rather than the rampant individualism of today, was the primary unit.

It is important to recognize that this is very different from the way we think today. Christopher Wright expresses this helpfully when he calls us to reorientate our perspective to be able to see things from an Old Testament point of view so we can become biblical (rather than just New Testament) Christians:

> We tend to begin at the personal level and work outwards. Our emphasis is to persuade people to live a certain kind of life according to this and that moral standard. If enough individuals live up to such-and-such a morality, then, almost as a by-product, society itself will be improved or at least maintained as a healthy, happy, safe environment for individuals to pursue their personal goodness. *This* is the kind of person you must be; *that* kind of society is a bonus in the background.[14]

This is certainly the dominant way of thinking in the modern Western church. A Christian nation would come about purely by personal evangelism and by demonstrating personal righteousness. But this approach is inadequate of itself. Social or structural righteousness is needed because of the reality of social or structural evil. Christopher Wright continues,

> The Old Testament tends to place the emphasis the other way round: here is the kind of society God wants. His desire is for a holy people for his own possession, a redeemed community, a model society through whom he can display a prototype of the new humanity of his ultimate redemptive purpose. Now if that is the kind of society God wants, what kind of person must you be once you belong to it?[15]

This does not mean of course that the individual is any less responsible. The individual implications of God's requirements of his people were obvious. If God wanted a society characterized by equality and respect for the poor then oppressing them by dishonestly making money out of them, or making any money at their expense, was unacceptable. Similarly the enjoinder to care for the alien (the ethnic minority group) has a very pointed significance in the modern context of our problems of race and racism. Such a set of problems will have both a social and a personal dimension. Structural racism must be campaigned against wherever it is found; personal racism must be shown to be incompatible with the gospel of reconciliation within the church, and part of that mockery of people which is an insult to the God who made them.

At this point it may be objected that it is all very well to quote from the Old Testament and to draw examples from the life of Israel, but surely the New Testament is entirely different. Jesus is concerned with personal salvation. He does not seem to be at all concerned about justice. Should not the church be more concerned with personal salvation and people's eternal security than with their economic well-being in this life? Much of the modern church behaves as if this were its point of view and it is important that we consider this. But we shall leave this to chapter nine, on the church, as it is important to see the life of the church and its relationship to society in the light of Jesus's teaching on the kingdom of God.

In this chapter we have looked at the foundations of all Christian belief, the revelation of the character of God. The God we worship is a God of justice as well as a God of love, mercy and peace. Not only is he a God of justice but his justice runs contrary to the secular justice of much of our modern world. God creates community and through his people he includes the poor and weak. They enjoy their rights and shalom, because they are made in God's image. The people of God guarantee the quality of their lives because they too recognize that they are no different from the poor, having been slaves themselves, delivered by the same act of justice which God asks them to perform. Their responsibilities to the poor underwrite the rights of the poor. Both are founded on God's character. Consequently God demands of his people that always and everywhere they be characterized by justice, for only thus will they be recognizable as the people of God. In a world which everybody, Christian or not, recognizes as containing blatant injustice, the people of God cannot choose only those aspects of God's character which they find most easy to emulate. A commitment to justice will mean being prepared for conflict and not just reconciliation. It will mean confrontation with the powerful and the oppressors. Sometimes it will mean confrontation between church and state.

Because God the Creator does not have two standards for his creatures, this model of justice is not only a model for the church but is God's model for the world. It is his wish that we should so order our societies that the poor are not excluded or treated *en bloc* by an anonymous system which creates dependency and alienation. Christians can never be satisfied with so-called solutions to the 'problem' of the poor which throw money at the 'problem'. This is not only paternalistic but it treats the 'poor' as a blot on the landscape which needs to be removed. The Christian cannot get away from the fact that God wishes poor people to be drawn into the same quality of relationships as the rest of the community.

This is a great threat to two categories of people whom we have already described. Firstly, the narcissist will find this message almost unbearable. Whatever his material state the narcissist regards his own problem as the major one. It is he who needs a bigger and more meaningful experience of God: healing, ecstasy, fellowship, blessing or affirmation. The idea that God is calling him to give himself to the poor is fundamentally antagonistic to his view of what faith is about. Christianity is for him and his own personal consumption, not for others.

Secondly, this message is anathema to those who subscribe to the culture of privacy. Their whole lives have been spent increasing their own control over their lives so that they could become more free to choose whom they will associate with. Such people regard 'the poor' as 'them' and as a threat to privacy rather than an opportunity for friendship. Thus they live the poorer in their shrinking world.

CHAPTER SEVEN

POLITICS AND COMPROMISE

So the church is likely to be attacked from both sides if it does its duty. It will be told that it has become political when in fact it has been careful only to state principles and point to breaches of them; and it will be told by advocates of particular policies that it is futile because it does not support these. If it is faithful to its commission it will ignore both sets of complaints and continue so far as it can to influence all agencies and permeate all parties.

WILLIAM TEMPLE

Democracy: The worst possible form of government, except for all the others that have been tried.

WINSTON CHURCHILL

Our new starting point is belief in a just God rather than in an idolatrous philosophy which does not refer to God. How does this work itself through in political terms? We have seen that our vision is of justice for the poor but if this vision is to be put into practice we must be willing to enter the political arena. From the outset we must be clear that a wide range of political beliefs are consistent with Scripture. Some people will choose to express their politics through joining a right-wing party, others will opt for a form of socialism.

Christians are committed to two things which come before our loyalty to any particular party and which define the limits of our loyalty. Firstly, all Christians should be committed to deriving their politics from Scripture. Secondly, at least in the West, we are committed to democracy, which has many imperfections but which, as Winston Churchill points out, is superior to most other forms of government if not all of them.

Everybody, including Christians, is involved in politics whether they like it or not. Politics is about the shape of the community we live in. In so far as those who govern can affect such things, it is about the values at the heart of our society and the vision of the future to which we aspire. Politics is also about the particular policies used as tools to sustain those values and bring about such a vision.

Involvement in politics does not just mean being involved in party politics. Anybody involved in the life of the community, enabling people to find resources to accomplish their goals, is involved up to the hilt. Anybody who uses the resources provided by the state is involved whether it be by using state-subsidized transport, being treated by state-subsidized health-care facilities or by buying a house with a mortgage on which income tax relief is given. We are all implicated in the life of the state, and, as we have seen, the state is heavily involved in our lives as well.

Those who decry involvement preferring to 'keep out of politics' are in fact making a deeply political statement. Onlookers presume that their lack of participation means that they are happy with things as they are. When Christians fail to participate, they give the impression that they are concentrating on their own piety to the exclusion of any real interest in the quality of other people's lives. Such silence is a massive vote for the *status quo*. Ironically it is usually such people who, when looking at the standards of contemporary society, see decadence and the need for change. The double irony is that their silence has contributed more to society's decadence than a thousand of the supposed conspiracies such people constantly seem to see in the world of politics. As the old saying has it, 'All that is necessary for evil to prevail is that good men do nothing', or as Martin Luther King once put it,

> He who passively accepts evil is as much involved in it as he who helps to perpetrate it.[1]

The role of the state

Sin needs constant restraint if the fabric of our civilization is not to crumble away completely. To aid us in this fight, God has given to us the gift of the state to order our lives. In Romans 13:1–7, Paul draws our attention to the role of the state as representing, in a limited way, God's justice within history.

In particular Paul tells us that we must submit to the governing authorities because they are established by God. Anarchy is rebellion against God because it rebels against his order in society. Rulers' power should be limited, for according to Paul they 'hold no terror for those who do right' (verse 3) but those who do wrong must remember that they 'do not bear the sword for nothing' (verse 4). The state has power under God to uphold good and punish wrong. When it functions in this way, the state does what God would do, and is therefore deserving of our 'respect' and 'honour' and should receive our 'taxes'.

There are occasions of civil disobedience in Scripture and this tradition is extremely important in the relationship of the Christian church to the state. Moses before Pharaoh;[2] Shadrach, Meshach and Abednego before Nebuchadnezzar;[3] Daniel before Darius;[4] Peter and John before the Sanhedrin[5] all 'obeyed God rather than men'. They were in a position where to obey the state (or in the case of Peter and John, the Jewish authorities), would be to disobey God.

Where the state attempts to take the place of God and demands that we do things which run clearly and directly in contradiction to God's own claim on our lives, then just as clearly the Christian has a mandate to disobey the state and obey God. In this situation the state is no longer the state of Romans 13 but the state of Revelation 13 (the beast from the sea), which demands idolatry from its followers. This state is no longer upholding good and punishing evil but has gone the way of the society described in Romans 1:32:

> Although they know God's righteous decree that those who do such things deserve death, they not only continue to do these very things but also approve of those who practise them.

The state which sanctions evil must be resisted at all costs. However, this is a long way from disagreeing with the policies of a government that does not happen to be to one's own liking. It is not for us to set ourselves up to say that whenever we disagree with a policy even on moral grounds we should commit civil disobedience. We should use every means at our disposal to persuade others of the strength of our case. But where other equally committed and biblical

Christians disagree with us we must be extremely careful. We do not live in a society where we have lost our freedom of expression because of the suppression of human rights. Those who believe that particular policies are morally wrong are those who must be most actively committed to reversing them.

The problem with politics

So far, so good. We are involved whether we like it or not and we must be discerning about government even though we have a responsibility to maintain it. It is important to recognize the importance of democracy which, though a fallen system like any other, has peculiar merits of its own. As Reinhold Neibuhr has commented,

> Man's capacity for justice makes democracy possible, but man's inclination to injustice makes democracy necessary.[6]

As Christians we are surely committed to democracy first, rather than to any specific party. The freedom of choice entailed in democracy rests on there being more than one option vigorously upheld before the general public. From the standpoint of those who uphold democracy the fact that there is a choice of two, three or four parties is no embarrassment save perhaps an 'embarrassment of riches'. To believe that one view of life should predominate and that all Christians should agree about what that view should contain is to hope for too much in a fallen world.[7]

However, it is not enough for Christians to represent opposite points of view with integrity; we are committed to the truth and we must therefore be constantly seeking to reconcile our views with those of others and with the perspective of Scripture, which is not politically neutral, for we worship a God of justice. It may well be that a political party will stray from a true Christian concern for the poor and oppressed or may suppress human rights to freedom in pursuing social policy. In that case it is up to the church along with Christian politicians and members of that party to bring it back to a knowledge of the truth.

Richard Neuhaus has said,

> Democracy is the appropriate form of governance in a fallen creation in which no person or institution,

> including the church, can infallibly speak for God. Democracy is the necessary expression of humility in which all persons and institutions are held accountable to transcendent purposes imperfectly discerned.[8]

He continues by saying,

> Of course democracy is unsatisfactory. All orders short of the kingdom of God are unsatisfactory. The discontents of democracy – its provisionality and incompleteness – are the signs of political health. The hunger for a truly satisfying way of putting the world in order is laudable. But that is a hunger for the kingdom of God, and it is dangerously misplaced when it is invested in the political arena.[9]

Christianity and politics

We have already seen that it is important to recognize that modern life is inextricably bound up with the political. We have also recognized that the political system in which we live offers us the maximum possible opportunity for expressing our own opinions and seeking to influence the political process. How are Christians to relate to the existence of the party political divide as it is represented in the West and most particularly in the UK?

Just as economics cannot be divorced from higher moral and religious values, so, as we have seen, our Christianity will be the most important factor in determining our politics.

> Every political theory is formed within the framework of a broader system of philosophy, from which it derives basic axioms and assumptions . . . The answers a writer gives to the questions 'what is ultimately real?', 'what is ultimately good?', and 'what can I know about the good and the real, and how can I know it?' are crucial . . .[10]

Christianity is a critical religion and views both systems of political philosophy as deeply provisional and secular. Politics asks searching questions of those who would give their time and talents to effecting change through a particular party. These are questions such as 'With whom do you identify?' or 'From where do you derive your beliefs and values?' The political activist who is not a Christian can give the standard answers without many problems. They identify with rich or poor: they derive their beliefs from John Stuart Mill and Milton Friedman or Marx and Lenin. I am over-simplifying for the purposes of illustration, but things are more complex for the Christian.

Because the Left has enshrined equity as the principle at the heart of its system and the Right has enshrined freedom as the value from which all other values have derived, Christians cannot be happy merely with loyalty to one system of thought. Our explanation of the tensions within the welfare state has already shown us that both of these principles are found in Scripture and both are important to human dignity, responsibility and community.

Why should Christians be constantly pushed into defining their politics in secular terms? If we believe the Bible is true and that the vision of human life it portrays is prior to any cultural arrangement for political life, then such a vision must judge our current political arrangements. Christians will not, therefore, be committed *en bloc* to any political party, but even where they are party members there will be a tendency to be critical of the party line in the name of their Christian faith (hence the quotation from William Temple at the head of this chapter).

Of course, the usual question to be asked at this point is: 'It is all very well to criticize the efforts of political parties to guide the nation but what are you going to put in its place?' Often the answer is seen to be some kind of third way which combines the best of both wings while leaving out their worst excesses. But whatever one's position on the Left-Right spectrum, that spectrum is one which has been defined in secular terms. All its mixes of political philosophy are secular even though they may be more acceptable to a majority of the voting population than other possibilities.

Christians surely recognize that in a fallen world politics will always be an arena for compromise, and, whatever its form, will be deeply inadequate and provisional. The realism of Scripture is its recognition that until Christ returns governments will continue to rise and fall and will exhibit different strengths and weaknesses. The church will relate the activity of such governments to the vision of justice and freedom contained in Scripture and will urge them on to greater efforts. But it is *Christianity* to which the church calls the people and not a 'new politics' defined in secular terms, even if this is couched in the language of a 'third way'.

It is important for this to be understood. I am not arguing for a return to the old pietistic individualism of past years where people hid from the claims of political life. I am arguing that the church must recover a corporate dimension which is deeply political but not *party political*. As part of its mission the church will always wish to show the world that where the kingdom of God is at work it is possible to transform the dynamics of society into something more pleasing to God. It will do this not only by infiltrating society and seeking to bring about creative reform through traditional political means, but it will also need to establish 'communities of hope' which can demonstrate the difference Christ makes.

Such a strategy is adopted when we recognize that though we must constantly confront the world in the name of Christ, we cannot change the whole world into the kingdom, and must live in a fallen world till Christ himself ushers it in. What we can do is set up small projects which are like candles in the darkness so that when people despair of the tawdry they can turn and see the light. Such projects will be extraordinarily diverse. They may include credit unions, old peoples' homes, welfare-rights work, mother and toddler groups, housing associations, self-help unemployment groups, soup kitchens, sheltered workshops and many other ideas. The point is that they are run according to Christian principles where those people whom the world renders powerless are given skills and the opportunity to participate in community. They are shown love and at the same time are given resources. It is made known that the reason this is being done is because God has shown us his love in Christ.

It is therefore important for the church to engage with the political world, for we must recognize that, as Michael Ignatieff has said:

> To be modern is to be discontented and to be discontented is to be political.[11]

As Christians we must recognize that such discontent is not just an expression of greed nor merely an expression of hunger for the material world. Modern discontent is a sign of spiritual homelessness; a longing for the kingdom of God. Our duty is two-fold. Firstly, we must provoke government of whatever colour to take small steps towards 'justice and righteousness' because God cares about his world. Secondly, the Christian church itself is meant to be the new community towards which men and women are pointed. But this concept of the church as the signpost of the kingdom of God is still only on the distant horizon. Until we can grasp a holistic vision for the church as a counter-community not only of traditional spirituality but also in terms of culture, economics, politics and social concern, we shall continue to be passed over much as we are now.

We shall look at this concept in more detail in the next chapter, but before doing that, it is important to look at some problems which face those who do feel called to engage in the political arena as an expression of their personal vocation.

The Christian in political life

When people enter political life they find that many of the decisions they are required to make are not straight choices between good or bad, right and wrong. Much of the time they are called to wrestle in areas where they may feel quite inadequate. This is as true of the person who becomes a parent governor for a local school as it is of local councillors or national politicians. In particular they face some problems which arise specifically because they are Christians. These are problems of authority, compromise, disagreement and expectations. These we shall now examine.

1. Imposing or persuading

One of the first questions people ask when they enter political life is *'What right do I have to impose my views on other people?'* The answer is, of course, 'None at all.' With regard to ideas and beliefs, the only right one has in a democracy is the right of persuasion. It is important that Christians should not only put forward the strongest possible case for their point of view, but also that they should attempt to defeat the strongest version of their opponent's point of view. How often one hears right-wingers comparing capitalist theory with socialist practice, or socialists comparing the idealism of socialism with the unacceptable face of capitalism. Integrity demands that we compare like with like. I have often seen Christians who lean to one political side or the other dismiss those who disagree with them or paint a caricature of the opposition which is so feeble that one wonders how anybody could accept it.

The challenge to Christians is to portray the strongest possible case for the opposition and *then* to knock it down. There is no virtue in knocking down a straw man. Many Christians who would subscribe to a socialist view of life completely underestimated the strength of Mrs Thatcher's arguments in her first two terms of office. Few took monetarism seriously and even fewer treated it with the respect it deserved. Although it was widely unpopular as a doctrine, Christian integrity demanded that it be taken seriously.

Such integrity comes with a commitment to democracy and to vigorous debate. It is important that we attempt to understand the opposition – not only the intellectual propositions behind their arguments but the emotional and personal background of those with whom we disagree. Democracy gives us the possibility of maintaining friendships with them.

There is one other factor in democracy which it is important to recognize. The expression of strong opinions and even of anger across the floor of Parliament is a strength from society's perspective and not a weakness. The fact that such exchanges can happen, that government authority can be questioned and ministers of the Crown be called to account for their actions is a feature of the open society to which we belong. The ability of a left-wing MP to debate with a right-wing leader without the country falling apart must bring some credit to the system. The problem comes not with the portrayal of angry exchanges in the 'House' but in those areas of our national life which are not democratically accountable.

2. The nature of compromise

The second problem is *the nature of compromise*, which we have already touched on. All too often Christians say that they do not wish to get involved because of the necessity of compromise. Of course if Christian truths were always discredited in political life it would be no place for the Christian. But this is not the nature of political compromise. As we noted above, this consists in getting the best possible deal in a fallen world given the political constraints at that time. As the old saying has it, 'In the absence of the best, pursue the better.'

> . . . compromise is not so much something we do as it is something we acknowledge. We acknowledge that the ordering of the world short of the kingdom of God *is* compromised.[12]

Politics has been called 'the art of the possible'. That is a statement of fact rather than of disillusioned cynicism. Christians need to see that both the ideals of the beatitudes and the 'horse trading' over policies are necessary to the Christian politician.

The ideals of the Christian faith spell out the answer to the question, 'What sort of society do we want?' Ultimately, of course, we want the kingdom of God to come, but unfortunately that is not a feasible political option! Keeping Christian ideals in view we need to take small steps towards them. Some will find progress too slow, while others might disagree with our methods.

Tim Sainsbury MP tells of the time when he came top of the ballot which meant he could introduce a Private Member's Bill into Parliament. He decided as an experienced politician to look at the Abortion Law. In his opinion, the only part of the law which had a chance of reform was the ruling permitting abortions up to the twenty-eighth week of pregnancy. Deciding to go ahead he went for support to some of the pro-life pressure groups.

They told him that they wanted the whole law repealed – it was all or nothing. He knew that was not possible, and moved on to something else. The problem was that the pressure groups did not understand the nature of political compromise. It does not mean compromising our faith or even our ideals, but merely getting the best possible option given the political climate of opinion.

> . . . the person who makes a compromise is making a moral judgement about what is to be done when moral judgements are in conflict.[13]

Of course there will be occasions when the choice is between two apparent evils rather than between good and evil, but this is no more true of politics than any other area of life. The Christian in public life is required to be a glowing witness to the truth and integrity of the gospel. If all of politics means affirming evil choices then that person's life can no longer be the testimony to Christ that it once was. Politics is no dirtier than the society which it serves.

All justice within history is at best approximate. This is a problem for idealists who always wish for more than is possible. Christians are (or rather should be) realistic because they accurately portray the extent of human sinfulness. They should, therefore, recognize the constraints on the politician who cannot govern either solely by power or by conformity to previous traditions. Politics is always and everywhere a compromise. As Oliver O'Donovan points out, for Israel, Moses was the mouthpiece of God's law, but for Jesus he was an agent of compromise ('Moses permitted you to divorce your wives because your hearts were hard. But it was not this way from the beginning.').[14] He says that

> . . . the exercise of political authority is the search for a compromise which, while bringing the fullest witness to the truth that can in the circumstances be borne, will nevertheless lie within the scope of possible public action in the particular community of fallen men which it has to serve.[15]

The fact that all policies are a compromise does not mean that they should not be supported. There is a paradox at the centre of all political authority. The law may require us to pay taxes to support government programmes which we think are immoral. However much we may disapprove of the policies we are still obliged to pay the taxes. The government's claim on us is to some degree independent of their particular policies. Government is preferable to anarchy. Jesus told his disciples to 'render unto Caesar the things that are Caesar's'. Caesar may not have been a good governor but paying taxes enabled the process of government to go on. The fact of government itself has a moral claim on us to which we are forced to submit even though we disagree with specific policies. Even the leader of the Opposition presumably pays his taxes!

The paradox is that this same Christian morality which leads me to conform to the government (to 'obey the authorities', Romans 13:1), also leads me to search for truth. The law may demand conformity but only the truth can foster obedience.

We can therefore pass judgment on what we are required to do in the light of the truth. This paradox is essential to any democracy worthy of the name. I both conform to the delegated power of God that has been given to the government, and obey the truth revealed by God by which we judge the actions of the government. So our conformity ensures that there is continuity in society. But the government's stance has to be constantly and critically scrutinized to prevent them from leading us in the wrong direction, in which case they should be voted out. If everybody acted on their own instinctive dislikes and disobeyed the law when they thought there was something wrong, anarchy would quickly result. Yet, on the other hand, if truth is not expressed, oppression is the result.

Those who see the ideals of the Christian faith as realizable within history rather than as criteria for assessing whether a society is on the right course or not, will always see politics as betraying its moral standards. Questions of relating practicality to principle will always be fraught with difficulties in our fallen world. But Christians are driven to wrestle with these problems because they are driven by love. Involvement in politics is not a dispassionate calling; it has as much to do with the stirring of the emotions as with intellectual resolve. The Christian in politics crusades to defend the weak, bring freedom to the oppressed and recovery of sight to the blind. Righteous anger, compassion, a passion for justice and most simply a love for people (not people in general but specific people with real needs), will always transform the most unpromising politicians into dynamite.

3. Differences of opinion

We have seen that one problem faced by the Christian in politics is that of authority (not imposition of ideas but the privilege of persuading in order to bring understanding). A second is that of compromise (the means by which Christians could move society towards Christian ideals). We must now turn to the third problem: *disagreement between Christians*.

Christians will always have more to unite them than to divide them. One of the great sadnesses of our day is that we seem to concentrate on what divides rather than on that which unites. This is due to the individualism rampant in our society. We may know what we believe as individuals but without identifying with corporate statements of the historic Christian faith.

The Christian mind is first and foremost a humble mind. It recognizes its own bias, prejudice and tendency towards sin. All these things are brought under the authority of Scripture and exposed by it. The Bible condemns racism, fascism, nationalism and sexism. Christians cannot discriminate between people on the basis of prejudice. Nor can they oppress the poor without insulting God the Creator.

If we are to reflect God's own priorities politically we must be willing to learn from the entire community, including brothers and sisters abroad. It is easy to dismiss liberation theology as Marxist nonsense from the safety of the leafy suburbs, but not so easy when talking to those deeply committed Christians who are involved in the struggle within their country. We must learn from one another in order to learn from Christ. If it is possible for Christians to demonstrate unity where the world expects disunity, then, even though there may still be a difference of opinion, that spirit of unity between the people will speak of Christ.

On 17 June 1986, in the House of Commons, three MPs rose to speak in the South Africa debate. They asked that their speeches be taken together. The only thing that was unusual about this was that they were from different parties. Alistair Burt (Conservative), Simon Hughes (Liberal) and Peter Pike (Labour) spoke together as 'brothers in Christ' referring to each other as 'honourable friends', a term usually reserved for members of the same party. The impact of this was considerable, showing plainly that their brotherhood in Christ was greater than their political differences.

It is important that whatever the area of our calling, we are agents of reconciliation. We should not be overly critical of the differences of politicians. More hurt has come to the body of Christ through the divisions perpetrated by church leaders than through the 'sound and fury' of politicians. Differences of opinion present opportunities for demonstrating reconciliation which is possible only through the moving of the Holy Spirit.

The problem of Christian disagreement is not unique to politics. It is also present among theologians! Again, as in the case of the other problems which we have already discussed, disagreement can provide a marvellous opportunity to show the difference which the Christian life makes. Firstly, Christians can show that they handle the *content* of their disagreement differently from others. Because they have a degree of humility they are willing to accept that others may be in the right. They also submit to Scripture and are willing to be shown that they must change their views because of what it says. Although Christian politicians will always hold their views with great passion they should be open and willing to listen in a way which may not be evident elsewhere.

Secondly, differences of opinion give an opportunity to show that the *manner* in which we deal with them is different. If Christ told Christians to love their *enemies*, then surely we can expect mutual respect and even deference between Christians who disagree only about political ideology or economic policy. Here again we see the application of the principle which was talked about in chapter two, that the love of God is most evident when it crosses the dividing lines and boundaries which the world erects. When people who fundamentally disagree over politics offer one another the love of God, then the world sits up and takes notice saying, 'See how they love one another.' Such love is not as evident between people whom the world expects to agree on other things because they agree about their politics. In politics as in the rest of life the cross and the behaviour of the Christian who carries the mark of the cross can turn potential problems into positive opportunities.

4. Law and morality

A further problem for those involved in politics is that even if all politicians were Christians, the laws they passed would not make people more moral. With this we must agree. Mankind will always be sinful. No amount of lawmaking can change the human heart. Lawmaking can, however, change both attitude and behaviour. People may well remain drunkards, and the law is powerless to prevent that. But the laws can be passed which restrict the age at which people can buy alcohol, and punish those who drink and drive. The law can both reflect the state of society and reform society. In 1967 the Abortion Law was changed and liberalized.

The changes reflected the values of the permissive society of the 1960s. In the 80s the climate changed so that a lot of people were behind attempts to reform that law.

It may well be true that 'you cannot legislate morality', but concern for politics reflects a concern for the community. Christians can influence the behaviour of that community by caring enough to hold up the ideals of the Christian faith and to move society towards them. In doing so, much wisdom will be needed. But each problem in politics is also an opportunity. At the end of the day creative reform through politics can make our society more pleasing to God. If we do not care about that, or about the conditions in which our friends and neighbours live, how can we claim to be obeying the great commandment to love God and our neighbour?[16]

In the previous chapters we have seen how our motivation for involvement is the character of God himself and that social action is a necessary part of discipleship if we are to obey the great commission and the great commandment. Now we find that democracy welcomes those with such a vision and invites us to persuade others of our case. What freedom we enjoy to affect our society for Christ! How shall we face our Lord if, having had the motivation, the example and the opportunity, we remained in our ghettos complaining about falling standards in our society and the seeming inability of government to do anything about injustice?

CHAPTER EIGHT

THE CHRISTIAN MIND

We find so many who think truth is on their side but precious few who are 'on the side of truth'.
SIR WILLIAM ODER

Most political sermons teach the congregation nothing except what newspapers are taken at the Rectory.
C. S. LEWIS

Christians are often accused of opting for the *status quo*. It is not that the *status quo* is necessarily wrong or evil, but that Christians are expected to have a clear sense of right and wrong, justice and injustice in any society. We are meant to be discerning otherwise we cannot be an influence for good. If we have soaked up the world's values as we grow up how can we form a counter-culture or be 'light shining in the dark?' Part of the distinctiveness of the Christian is that his or her thinking is different.

Each of us faces perplexing questions in our working lives. Whether they are the ethical problems that face the businessman, or the political problems faced by teachers, housing officers or even doctors, there are certainly many questions that cause Christians to ask, 'What is the right and the good thing to do in this situation?'

Nor are such problems restricted to the professional world. Those who buy and sell houses for profit, for example, should always ask whether what they are doing is speculative and harmful to others or part of God's calling on their lives. Those who tacitly support the existence of credit cards by using them should at least ask whether they are enforcing the debt trap. Shoppers for cosmetics face questions over the animal experimentation that goes into producing make-up. The young unmarried woman who is pregnant will face an agonizing decision over the question of abortion. An unemployed person offered the chance of making some spare cash in the black economy will also be confronted by a tough decision.

Other questions face us all. The care of our elderly. To vote or not to vote? How to vote? Our duty to the poor in our area. Dealing with racial discrimination or sexism. The problems posed by ambition and the desire for power. Child abuse. Unemployment. Pollution. The potential guilt caused by affluent Western lifestyles. How are we to take a view on these things? How are our opinions to be formed?

Is Scripture so indirect and vague that we can justify any position and feel comfortable that we are doing the right thing? It is a defensive measure to restrict our Christianity to 'spiritual' things and not to let our Christian faith inform these vital decisions which both shape us as people and indicate how far we are willing to go in following our faith. But how can we be sure that what we believe is Christian? What we believe is our guide to how we act and who we are.

Life is constantly throwing up questions which we may not even be able to articulate. In many cases we may have got no further than feeling uncomfortable about certain situations but not knowing why. We may be vaguely aware of subjects such as 'ethics' or 'moral philosophy' but the idea that these abstract, ivory-tower speculations could be helpful to a concerned shopper in the supermarket seems ludicrous.

Recognizing world-views

At the beginning of his film *Annie Hall* Woody Allen tells the following story directly to camera. Two elderly women are eating dinner in a restaurant in the Catskill mountains. One turns to the other and says, 'The food in this place is really awful.' The other replies, 'Yes, and there's so little of it.' Woody Allen comments that life is much like that. Most of it is awful but there is so little of it.

In another Woody Allen film, *Love and Death*, the character Boris pursues his cousin and finally gets her into bed where she starts philosophizing about the problems of the universe. As he advances to attempt to seduce her she exclaims, 'Oh Boris, sex without love is a meaningless experience!' To which he replies, 'Yes, but as meaningless experiences go, it's one of the best.'

Woody Allen's preoccupation with sex, death and the uncertainties of life are matched only by his neurotic self-absorption centred on his analyst and his demand that God give him a sign to show him that he exists. The following extract from *Without Feathers* has a serious side:

> . . . how can I believe in God when just last week I got my tongue caught in the roller of an electric typewriter? I am plagued by doubts. What if everything is an illusion and nothing exists? In that case I have definitely overpaid for my carpet. If only God would give me some clear sign! Like making a large deposit in my name at a Swiss bank.[1]

Woody Allen's world is one at which we laugh frequently. His obsession with sex, death, uncertainty and self reflects many of our own unspoken obsessions. His world-view is consistent. It is instantly recognizable. His movies are his interface with the world through which he projects his *Angst*. We are entertained. Yet his world-view is fundamentally antagonistic to Christianity. It elevates doubt rather than faith. It glories in introspection as reasonable. Neurosis is a rational response to a meaningless world. Sex is escapism, not a responsible commitment. Death is devoid of hope. Woody Allen's characters are so obsessed with self that they could never see God. His whole world is distorted even though he puts himself over as the person asking honest questions of life.

We too have a view of the world. We have adopted it from others (for we brought nothing into the world), and adapted it over the years for our own use. Using it, we sort out life into the important and the unimportant. Often we are not aware of our own judgments. We may believe that our view of the world is common sense and be amazed to find anybody to whom our views are like a red rag to a bull. It is because many of us do not hold very extreme views on anything that we imagine that what we believe instinctively about most things is at least compatible with Scripture even if it is not directly derived from Scripture. How many of us have come out from watching a Woody Allen film laughing or crying, without it having crossed our minds that as Christians we should disagree with him?

Many of us equate anything which is placed into the entertainment 'box' as something which we accept uncritically. We talk about 'switching our brains off' when we sit in front of the telly night after night, not realizing that we become what we feed on.

After all, if we had spent a comparable amount of time listening to a sermon or reading the Scriptures, we would expect to have been granted greater understanding of life.

For most of us our view of the world is not an academic thing. Our convictions are not based on a thorough reading of the entire works of Lenin and Marx or Milton Friedman or Jean-Paul Sartre. Indeed we would expect a Christian for whom those thinkers were important influences to have thought very carefully about the compatibility of such thinking with their Christian faith! Many of us are most influenced by our parents. Our own views are a mixture of theirs and our own struggle to achieve independence. We are also influenced by our peer group and by the personalities we grew up with. Who were the heroes whom we wished to emulate as children, adolescents and young adults? We are influenced by the expectations built into us by education and class. We have a view of what is 'normal' and it requires a great deal to take us beyond it in our commitments.

We are all affected by Western culture which many of us take in with the air we breathe as if it were natural and (more dangerously) 'neutral'. Our views on sexuality, money, spirituality, work, prejudice and reward often go unchallenged, with the possible exception of those who engage in verbal fisticuffs during the luxury of their student years. The rest of us ebb and flow with the tide of important responsibilities: birth, courtship, marriage, divorce, promotion, redundancy, disease, success, failure, retirement and death. The fact is that our distinctiveness as Christians on those issues which the non-Christian world considers to be important can quickly disappear.

The transformed mind

Yet our claim is that commitment to Christ does not allow us the luxury of settling down cosily with the world. Paul states,

> Do not conform any longer to the pattern of this world,
> but be transformed by the renewing of your mind.[2]

Peter writes,

> Always be prepared to give an answer to everyone who
> asks you to give the reason for the hope that you have.[3]

Earlier in the letter Peter exhorts us to 'prepare your minds for action'.[4] Paul, in relation to spiritual gifts and the importance of understanding what God, through the Holy Spirit, wants to say to his people, writes,

> Brothers, stop thinking like children. In regard to evil, be infants, but in your thinking be adults.[5]

Having 'the mind of Christ' is not automatic. When we become Christians we bring all kinds of baggage with us. Very little of our thinking, if any, will have been influenced by the claims and example of Christ. How are we to mature, to 'grow up'? Of course the Holy Spirit is given to us in order to guide us and reveal Christ to us, but the Bible says that we are to use our minds as well. This is not an optional command for intellectuals. Nor does it necessarily mean a flight to piles of books and theories. It simply means that God demands that all of our life be given over to him.

When asked which was the greatest commandment in the law, Jesus replied,

> ' "Love the Lord your God with all your heart and with all your soul *and with all your mind*." This is the first and greatest commandment.'[6]

As we seek to renew our thinking and to bring the whole of life under the Lordship of Christ there are many traps for the unwary. God is not asking us to perform an academic exercise in order to win his favour. We are saved by his grace towards us and only by that.

All of a Christian's life is a response to God's gracious initiative. Our worship is a response to his self-revelation, our evangelism is a response to receiving his message of salvation for all people. Likewise our renewed thinking is a response to God as he opens up the new horizons of the kingdom of God. We want to live differently in obedience to him. We want to become more like Christ. Therefore, we want to think differently – about everything. This is not a drudging chore like studying for an exam. It is a voyage of discovery which we start here and continue for eternity in the presence of a God who by his nature is continually creating new things for us to explore.

Because of this, renewed thinking must lead to renewed action. God asks us to be 'transformed'. He does not ask us to take copious notes to file away and forget. We should then be like those who regard the 'filling of the Spirit' as an experience they had so many years ago ('I had it in 1978') and who have bottled it like a vintage wine. We need the infilling of the Holy Spirit *daily* if we are to be transformed. God wants us to challenge the world's thinking daily in our mind, our family, work and church, and to confront the world with truth. Once we start to do this we shall find it exhilarating.

Abstraction and distraction

Many people may object that they do not think conceptually or abstractly. Opening books to work out a Christian position on nuclear weapons would send them to sleep even if they were interested in doing it. Their world is the world of popular culture. Surely if 'the Christian mind' means intellectual rigour then this is just another form of elitism within Christianity. It will also quickly turn into a 'guilt trip' – yet another duty that Christians ought to be carrying out, and are not.

Each person living in our industrial society needs to be able to interpret it for themselves and become critically aware of it. This process is as much evident in the atmosphere in the senior common room as it is in gossip and in quarrels, in conversations on street corners, or when waiting together at the school gates to pick up the children. Each person, whatever his or her educational background, has a view of a complex society which makes sense to him or her and which he defends to members of his or her community. This belief is at the heart of dignity and a sense of responsibility for one's actions. It is the image of God in all of us that makes us want to take responsibility for our actions. The fact that a person's world-view is 'informal' does not necessarily mean that it conforms to worldly thinking.

Conformity implies a passive acceptance of what is going on. One is a follower and not a shaper of society. The Scriptures tell us that we are to be 'conformed to the image of his Son' and that we are not to be 'conformed to this world but transformed . . .' In other words we are not passively to accept the world's way of doing things but are to seek to become like Christ. *This means that Christianity is a critical force in society.*

Because God's revelation is given from outside history it stands over the events of history and judges them. But because God has graciously revealed himself within history the development of Christianity is inescapably part of history itself and must be self-critical as well. It is therefore important for Christians not only to think critically about those affairs happening 'in the world' but also to inquire to what extent the Christian church has become socially and personally conformist rather than an agent of change.

The church will be conformist when Christians spend most of their time looking at the lives of other Christians (the normality versus normativity debate of an earlier chapter). If one's subconscious aim is to blend in with the crowd and to derive one's identity as a Christian from being like them, it follows that the call to be distinctive will pose a fundamental threat. Though Christians may applaud such a call they may well fail to make any personal response.

It may be that such people are *au fait* with all conceivable positions which Christians can adopt with biblical integrity on issues as diverse as nuclear war or AIDS. But if, at the end of their debate, they close their notebooks and do not act, they cannot be said to be either 'transformed' or 'renewed'. The accumulation and de-accumulation of knowledge which passes for wisdom in the world is not wisdom in the Christian sense. To the Hebrew mind, for instance, one could not be said truly to 'know' something until one had put it into action. Those who have little formal education but who loves the Lord and know the Scriptures may sometimes have a clearer vision of what needs to be done to change the world than those intellectuals who prevaricate endlessly.

Christian wisdom or Christian mind?

Many prefer to see knowledge as something learnt through apprenticeship. Jesus did not give his disciples a pile of books and tell them to come back when they had developed a Christian mind. He took them with him and they learnt from him directly. When one learns from books there still remains a gap between knowing and doing. Fear can strike the would-be evangelist as she or he tries to put the bookwork into practice. But the person who is taken along by another evangelist and who learns by doing, also learns to conquer his or her fear as part of the learning process. Today there seem to be so few people who are making apprentices of others so that they can learn on the job. A Christian mind does not need to be daunted by books for what it gains may be more like wisdom than knowledge.

It is important that the idea of 'the Christian mind' or of 'thinking Christianly' does not become an excuse for elitism within the church. It often seems that those who talk most about the Christian mind are those who have the most stringent intellectual standards. The impression can be given that unless one is willing to analyse a particular social issue in depth with all the facts at our disposal and with a good grasp of biblical theology, our beliefs are not as valuable as they could be. This places an intolerable burden on people who do not share an analytical calling.

When I was a young boy there were elderly people in the church where I worshipped who could hardly read or write but who could talk wisely about the world in which they lived. Of course it was a small world, an island community and, some would say, a very insular community. Nevertheless they were wise about that world. Such wisdom had not come from books but from perceptions of life itself. Often it would come in the form of stories or of sayings which were easily understood and passed down from parent to child. The important thing about this wisdom was that it had been gleaned in the process of living and was not abstracted from the real world. It was 'wisdom to live by'.

The wisdom literature of the Bible largely consists of easy-to-remember proverbial sayings which are practical shorthand reminders about the way to live. If our Christian thinking does not change our way of life, either as individuals or as nations, it could be accused of being something of a luxury.

The need for analysis

Having said all this it is ironic that *the opposite is also true*. There is a powerful, anti-intellectual movement today, not least among students. We need those who can understand the complex and the intricate things of this world. It is also important to stress that those who have been given intellectual gifts and the ability to sift data and think conceptually are disobedient to their calling if they are lazy and do not attempt to use those gifts in order to interpret the world.

We need informed 'watchmen' in the professions to warn us of what is coming. Such people need to be on the frontiers of professional life. In many professions we are faced with ethical problems of enormous proportions and too few people are thinking through these issues from a Christian standpoint.

So, whether our views are expressed in stories and experiences or in academic papers and 'café debate', the question at issue is whether what we believe accords with the Scriptures, and if it does, whether we are willing to do something about it.

Preparing our minds for action

How can we approach issues so that we shall be transformed not only as individuals but also as a church? This process must derive from a correct and complete use of the Bible. Many of us use the Bible for our personal devotions and apply it to our daily lives, but we do not see that the Bible also gives us both a macro-framework within which we can view these issues, and also new perspectives from which we can discover the truth.

In the light of what we have said already about the Bible speaking into the lives and situations of real people it is important to distinguish between 'perspectives' and 'principles'. Often those who are committed to Christian thinking look for principles derived from Scripture which can help us to understand a modern social phenomenon. Sometimes such principles do not exist. Where they do, the constant tendency is for them to take on a life of their own so that we soon refer to them without reference to God or his purposes. More often our Christian faith gives us a new set of perspectives on the world. These show us the direction in which we should be going but they may not show us exactly how we should do things. Much is left to us to decide before God.

In the area of ecology, for instance, Christians have a perspective which relies on the fact that God is the Creator and that we are trustees of his world. This is a powerful perspective which generates a great deal of thought and may even be helpful in forming policy. But it is not an abstract principle. It is a part of the Christian's world-view.

Our transformed perspective can continue only as long as we fix our eyes on God himself. It has no tendency to take on a life of its own.

The turning points of history

The Bible contains four great turning points in history from God's perspective. Only when we view the problems of man, nature and history in the light of these can we be sure that our perspective on life is not distorted. They are creation, the fall, redemption and consummation.

Creation

The creation story tells us many things which are directly contrary to the world's way of thinking. It tells us that we are made by God, in the image of God, for God. In other words our origins, our value and our purpose are all defined by this single event. Any point of view which regards mankind as an accident, or a result of the throw of cosmic dice, is contrary to Scripture. We are at the pinnacle of creation. Not only this but men and women together reflect the image of God. God's command to be trustees of his world and to be fruitful and multiply is given to men and women together. We are to fulfil our potential and to be creative. Notice though that the only thing that was not good prior to the fall was man alone. We are meant to live in community because God intended us to enjoy each other. Interdependence not independence is the norm, as we commented earlier. Here is the starting point for a critique of all those elements of modern Western individualism to which we are subjected today.

Whether we are looking at the role of men and women in society, the nature of work of the debate on the environment, the creation story will inform us and give us a starting place which reflects God's original intentions for his world.

The fall

The story of the fall can be found in two complementary passages. Genesis 3 tells the story of how our wilfulness led to our relationship with God being disrupted. It is not just a story about Adam and Eve; the fact is that the name of any individual born since then could be inserted and we would still have acted in the same way. The acts of the fall are replicated in millions of lives every day.

Four relationships were dislocated. Firstly, mankind died spiritually. The conscience and psychological well-being of men and women became distorted by evil. Mankind's sense of its own value, which was dependent on God, began to deteriorate. Secondly, our relationship with God was disrupted and we no longer worshipped our Creator or worked in harmony with him. Thirdly, our relationship with each other was disrupted and community began to disintegrate. Murder and hatred stole on the scene. Fourthly, our relationship with the environment changed. The animals began to fear people. The environment did not yield its fruit as easily, and God's gift of pastoral dominion became an exercise in domination leading to the exploitation of the earth's resources.

In this world the image of God is distorted. Relationships intended for mutuality and enjoyment become power relationships. People begin to justify themselves. Self-righteousness becomes a new religion. Idolatry replaces the worship of God.

We now live in a world where the only thing considered absolute is relativity itself. When Christians take a strong view of the fall we shall be realistic about the possibilities of moral progress apart from God's gracious intervention. We shall find ourselves disagreeing fundamentally with the Marxists and the humanists who believe that if only the social structures can be corrected, people will attain perfection.

The second passage describing the effects of the fall is Genesis 11:1–11, the story of the tower of Babel. This story graphically portrays people co-operating to do evil. If Genesis 3 recounts the story of individual acts of rebellion, Genesis 11 describes corporate or structural evil. Here was a community so fixed in its ambition to build a monument to its own glory that it built an immensely strong structure from bitumen and brick fired in the kiln, rather than dried in the sun as was common. These people wanted 'to make a name for themselves'. Rather than accepting the name and place which God had given to them they wanted to be 'self-made' men and women. They thought that this exercise would prevent them from being scattered over the earth. They hoped to control their own destiny. They were united in pride. At the heart of the ziggurat they constructed was probably a shrine to an idol. Their ambition as creators was to take over the place of God. People would worship their god instead.

Perhaps there is a parallel with the skyscrapers which dominate our Western skylines as a monument to the power of money and to the personalities that own them. When God brings his justice and glory they will be turned into follies.

Notice that no individual is responsible for building Babel. It is a corporate venture. They encourage one another in it. But this does not stop the community coming under judgment. Because of his mercy, God destroys the tower and scatters the people, confusing their language. If they had been allowed to follow their own path they would never have discovered God's best for their lives but would have collaborated in more gross acts of evil. As always God's judgment within history brings with it the possibility of a return to him and a new start. The tower is named Babel (meaning 'confusion'). Later Babylon (Gate of God) is established which is the city of oppression. The only thing built high in Babylon are its sins which are 'piled up to heaven'.[7]

It is important to realize that evil can be built in to the very culture and customs of a nation. We can speak of various past (and present) civilizations as 'cruel and despotic' not because compassionate individuals did not exist within them, but because evil ran throughout the culture. So we must be careful that our culture, laws and social norms reflect the highest achievable good.

The fall and its impact have implications for individuals and societies on issues as diverse as human rights, the need for the defence of a nation, crime and its restraint, exploitation of the poor, racism, pollution and pornography. Indeed there is no issue in which we are involved which is not in some way distorted by its impact. In his fight against all that is good and all that is of God, Satan most loves to use those instruments which we consider to be 'neutral'. If his approach were always heralded with trumpets, God's people would not need discernment. The fact is that if we are not to be wrong-footed we need to develop Christian thinking in every area of life.

Whenever a realistic moral assessment of human action is needed it is important to have a strong view of the fall. Where people are tempted to be romantic about the possibilities for any programme of human action the Christian must suggest that the possibility of failure must be allowed for and that safeguards must be built into the exercise. Christians are not surprised by sin, greed and injustice. They are saddened and angered by it. They fight and pray against it, but they are rarely surprised by it. When coups succeed and idealists take over a government, Christians wait to see whether revolution means change or whether power corrupts because all men and women are fallen and prone to succumb to temptation.[8] As Christians then, we are called to be biblical realists rather than naive optimists.

Redemption

Redemption is the process in history by which God has 'bought back' his people out of slavery. In redemption God graciously reveals himself in his great saving acts, and his people respond to him. Beginning with Abraham and continuing through the modern church age until the second coming of Christ, God is forming for himself a new community which will people the new creation.

We have already seen something of how God revealed himself in righteousness and justice, and also how Israel responded to that revelation when they obeyed the law. In fact not only the patterns and lessons of the law, but the prophets, the history, the psalms, wisdom literature, apocalyptic, the gospel of the kingdom, incarnation, atonement, resurrection and the example of the early church are there to enable us to glean an understanding not only of how we may live justly and love mercy but also of how we may influence for good the societies in which we have been placed.

Modern social issues are not new. They present, in new guises, problems which have faced mankind since the beginning of time. Even problems which appear to us to be very recent, such as our capacity to destroy the world by nuclear explosion, are paralleled in Scripture.

We do not worship a neutral God who looks benignly on all that we do. This is his world and many of the great issues of our day are laced with moral dilemmas. One of the great deceits of secularization is the conviction that not only is history heading nowhere but that the spiritual world has no influence on it.

At the centre of history stands the cross of Christ. All previous history was a preparation for it; all history since can be correctly seen only in its light. The message and the accomplishment of the cross should not be reduced to its work in the life of the individual believer. On the cross Christ was 'reconciling the world to God'. As we have already observed, the fall disrupted four relationships; that of people to God, human relationships, our relationship to self and our relationship to the environment. When Christ died he was healing and redeeming all those relationships and opening up the way for a new world where justice and righteousness, peace and joy were at the heart of human community. All that we do now in social and political action as well as in evangelism must carry the mark of the cross. The politician and the economist too are called to discover what it means to do what they do by the way of the cross. The cross is not something we value only in our personal and private spiritual life. By demonstrating victory through innocent powerlessness the cross shows us a pattern which Christians have a responsibility to weave through the whole fabric of life. To restrict the power of the cross is to rob the world of hope.

History is a battleground for vast spiritual forces. Principalities and powers fight for supremacy. Innocuous historical events may result from spiritual warfare. Christians are therefore to fight. We are saved to struggle, waging war with the whole armour of God. How little influence we have been persuaded we actually have! We look at politicians and wonder at their power, but from God's perspective the prayers of a Christian can change the world. Not only are we called to struggle but we are called to struggle in hope. We are not called to dark pessimism. Living as we do in the period between the first and second comings of Christ, we live by faith in what we shall soon experience at first hand.

As we commented earlier, all longing for perfection is a longing for the kingdom of God to come. To pretend that it is achievable within history is to deny the ravages of the fall. To deny that it will ever come is to succumb to a counsel of despair which robs the cross of its triumph and the Christian of hope. Whatever issues and problems we face it is necessary for this uncomfortable balancing act to be present.

Consummation

There will come a day when every eye will see that Jesus Christ is Lord. Justice will be done. Suffering will cease. Virtue will be rewarded. We shall worship God as he really is. Our faith will be purified from all selfish motives and we shall do by nature those things which please him. No barriers will exist to true human fellowship. The gathering of heaven represents all races and language groups, and both sexes. The best of our cultures will be brought into the new Jerusalem, purified from their worldliness. God will create again a new world in which righteousness dwells. In that world justice will not be needed in the same way as in ours. There will be no need for structures and laws to bring back a wayward community for the law will be written on our hearts and we shall do it gladly.

Since this is what all history strains towards, should we not dwell on it and seek to live its values now? If suffering does not exist there, should not we who belong to heaven bring relief from suffering here? If justice is done there should we not be the people of justice here? If the heart of heaven is the 'Lamb slain' should we not live lives given up for others?

All that we are taught to aspire to through self-interest in our Western culture already belongs to Jesus, the Lamb of God, because he put self-interest to death on the cross. His death was his greatest accomplishment. How contrary to all that the world stands for!

> 'Worthy is the Lamb, who was slain,
> to receive power and wealth and
> wisdom and strength
> and honour and glory and praise!'[9]

The list sounds like the aims of many a business school graduate! The world seeks these things to cover its nakedness. But for those who have eyes to see, the emperor has no clothes on! As Jesus repeatedly said, these things belong to those who have given away their lives.

If we, as Christians, are to recover our prophetic insight and courage, they will come when we can look at the events of history and see the spiritual dimension behind them. We shall then be able to call the world's bluff and rid ourselves of its hold on us. Then we shall know, as David did, that 'the Lord protects the simple-hearted'[10] – not the simple-minded, but the person who is so taken up with following God in every area of life that he or she has a clarity of insight which is not given to those who settle for inactivity in the face of complex issues. The simple-hearted are the clear-sighted; they have their priorities right in a world of distortion. The exciting news is that having a mind like Christ is not a duty for intellectuals but the joyful privilege of every Christian.

The mark of the Christian in the world is the cross. The four turning points of biblical history centre on the cross. The Lamb is worthy because he died. Without the cross creation is wasted, evil triumphs, redemption is powerless and consummation withers in a futureless despair. If we do not allow the influence of the cross to pervade our thinking, we shall quickly begin to slide into selfism and self-interest, moderation and 'normality', routine and finally boredom within our orthodoxy. Can it be said of us as it was of the apostles arriving in Thessalonica that we 'have turned the world upside down'? If we let God-directed thinking become our daily guide, it can happen still.

CHAPTER NINE

THE SIGNPOST TO THE KINGDOM

She say, Celie, tell the truth, have you ever found God in church? I never did. I just found a bunch of folks hoping for him to show. Any God I ever felt in church I brought in with me. And I think all the other folks did too. They came to church to share God not find God.

ALICE WALKER

Religion is the apex of man's rebellion against God.

KARL BARTH

The idea of the kingdom of God is fundamental to Jesus' own understanding of his ministry. Mark tells us that he came 'preaching the kingdom of God'. This has usually been understood by Evangelical Christians to mean the Lordship of Jesus Christ in the inner life, the personal rule of Jesus in the life of the believer. More recently the reign of God has been applied by social radicals to include his influence over all of life including the realms of politics, economics and society. The debate will no doubt continue between those who see it as personal and those who see it as social, but a new consensus is emerging which views the kingdom as both.

One of the reasons for the dichotomy which has existed for so long between those who see the kingdom in personal terms and those who interpret it in social terms has been the general division of life into the private and the public, which we discussed in chapter three.

Many people would say that Christians' involvement in political life is not spiritual, whereas evangelism is a spiritual activity. But if one accepts the Lordship of Jesus Christ over every realm of life, any activity which is done in his name and in obedience to him is spiritual. (The word 'spiritual' has almost completely lost its meaning and is frequently used as a synonym for 'emotional' or even 'ethereal'. Interestingly, a similar fate has befallen the word 'social'. Neither word is immediately clear any longer, but rather needs to be explained.)

The idea that we could restrict the kingdom to something which happens within a person is reductionist, to say the least. Membership of the kingdom of God will indeed have radical implications for the life of the believer but this is only one aspect of kingdom life. The richness of the picture which Jesus chose is that it is so multi-faceted.

Not only is the inner life changed but relationships between people are transformed. Galatians 3:28 tells us, 'There is neither Jew nor Greek, slave nor free, male nor female, for you are all one in Christ Jesus.' The old power relationships have passed away and we are all one in the kingdom of God. These new relationships are reflected in the new community of the church, so much so that the young church was heavily criticized by the Jewish authorities of the day for its laxity. But these new relationships and the new community were evidence that the new age had broken into the old. By his death, resurrection and ascension, Jesus had inaugurated the new age with its new values, new life in the Spirit and its hope of consummation when Christ would come again.

The idea of the kingdom or the rule of God was not new but reflected an important strand of thought within the Old Testament. The Old Testament writers looked forward to the day when God's reign would be acknowledged by everybody, his people vindicated and the nations judged. Jesus took this longing for God to appear and transformed it by his own interpretations and meaning. He himself, in his person and in his miracles, was the greatest sign that the kingdom had come, and in the personal miracle of his Messiahship, the resurrection, he made the kingdom secure.

Christians at the end of the twentieth century live, as did the disciples, between the 'already' and the 'not yet' of the kingdom. Although it is among us now and we live in it by faith, it has not yet fully replaced the old age. The division between the old and the new was not to be the final judgment but the coming of Christ.

When John the Baptist heard of what Jesus was doing while he was in prison, he sent his disciples to ask whether Jesus was the

Messiah or whether somebody else was still to be expected. Maybe he, like some of the disciples, expected the Messiah to deliver Israel from the hand of the Roman oppressor in a more tangible way. He had to learn, as did the disciples, that Jesus' kingdom was 'not of this world'. This does not mean that it is ethereal, having no social dimensions or implications, nor does it mean that the kingdom exists in the mind, which would imply that Christianity is merely a set of changed attitudes. Jesus' reply shows that his kingdom brings radical transformation into the lives of individuals and a radical challenge to the society in which he was living.

> Jesus replied, 'Go back and report to John what you hear and see: The blind receive sight, the lame walk, those who have leprosy are cured, the deaf hear, the dead are raised, and the good news is preached to the poor.'[1]

In saying this Jesus shows that the kingdom is not just about the extent of God's reign. Since God is Creator, Sustainer and Judge, the kingdom extends over the totality of human history and beyond it. Jesus demonstrates this by his authority not only over nature, but also over demons and also in his forgiveness of sins. Jesus thus shows that the reign of God is also about the power of God over his creation.

There are people today who, like Simon Magus in the Acts of the Apostles, desire the power of God without its ethical dimensions. But the power of the kingdom is available only to those who are obedient. Just as in the book of Amos, where we learn that the worship of God's people is not acceptable unless they reflect God's ethical requirements, so in the New Testament the values and the pattern of 'kingdom living' cannot be divorced from the power of God.

So much of the modern-day emphasis on God's power being available for the individual believer neglects to point out that that power is most evident when God's people reflect his values. But such values are sharply at odds with those of the world. Indeed becoming a member of the kingdom of God will turn one's world upside down!

Jim Wallis says of the sermon on the mount that it is the 'declaration of the kingdom of God, the charter of the new order'. He comments that the things that are so opposite to the description of the kingdom are the things we seek most eagerly. He concludes that the values of the kingdom are utterly incompatible with our own values and the way of the world.

> The Kingdom indeed represents a radical reversal for us. Aggrandizement, ambition, and aggression are normal to us and to our society. Money is the way to success. Competition is the character of most of our relationships, and violence is regularly sanctioned by our culture as the final means to solve our deepest conflicts. The scriptural advice 'Be anxious for nothing' challenges the heart of our narcissistic culture, which, in fact, is anxious over everything. To put it mildly, the Sermon on the Mount offers a way of life contrary to what we are accustomed. It overturns our assumptions of what is normal, reasonable, and responsible. To put it more bluntly, the Sermon stands our values on their heads.[2]

This applies not only to difficult personal relationships but also to the whole question of liberation and poverty which was so important for many of the people who heard Jesus tell his kingdom parables. One reason the kingdom represents an alternative pattern of living and not just a set of 'blessed thoughts' is that it contains an option for the poor which is repeatedly emphasized by Jesus, both in his own personal behaviour and in his teaching.

Those who claim that Jesus never got involved in politics forget that the religious authorities of the day were the oppressors. On many of the pages of the gospels Jesus is found denouncing, disagreeing with or exposing the religious authorities. At his trial he called into question the assumption of the political rulers of his day (Pilate and Herod) that their power entitled them to impose their will on others. He also taught that becoming a member of the kingdom implied giving up wealth to the poor and he condemned those rich oppressors who were unwilling to do so.

Jesus' own relationships with certain people posed a fundamental threat to the social structure of Jesus' day which was upheld by religious bigotry and prejudice. When Jesus ate with publicans or affirmed Zaccheus the tax collector as 'a son of Abraham', and when he accepted the anointing from the prostitute woman or talked with a Samaritan woman by the well, he overturned established conventions and posed a threat to the way society was organized. The results are summed up in the behaviour of the early church expressed in the verse we have already quoted, Galatians 3:28.

For Jesus, true religion as expressed in Luke 4:18–22, meant liberation from oppression and good news for the poor. His denunciation of the religious authorities was not just because of hypocrisy, but because they increasingly saw religion as a form of impossible bondage which ordinary people could not possibly hope to escape. It had become a kind of elitism in which only the intellectual Pharisee could flourish; a tangled web of rules and regulations rather than 'the glorious liberty of the children of God'.

Jesus' teaching on the kingdom showed that his was a kingship which arrives by joy:

> The kingdom of heaven is like treasure hidden in a field. When a man found it, he hid it again, and then in his joy went and sold all he had and bought that field.[3]

Jesus shows that the response to the presence of the kingdom is a joyous reaction to the discovery of God's grace. It is certainly not a dutiful burden. One of our problems today is that we see the power of God and of the kingdom as a gracious gift from God while seeing the requirements of the kingdom and its option for the poor as a threat to our material existence. We thus show that we do not believe that the way of life described in Jesus' kingdom parables is the very best that we could have. In so far as we look to the kingdom for 'spiritual power' and to the world for 'material security' we are trying to have our cake and eat it.

In Matthew 6:33 Jesus says in the beatitudes, 'Seek first his kingdom, and his righteousness.' Stephen Mott in his book *Biblical Ethics and Social Change* comments,

> This commitment to and longing for the triumph of God's will is the basis of the prayer, 'Thy kingdom come, They will be done, On earth as it is in heaven'.[4] We are to choose our ultimate allegiance and then to be zealous in it. And we seek not only the Reign, but also the justice that belongs to it.[5]

When we begin to appreciate the extent to which God wishes our behaviour to be different from that of the world we also begin to realize the extent of the kingdom community.

Modern Christianity easily preaches repentance as an entrance requirement of the kingdom. But to yearn after justice as an expression of the reign of God is to ask questions not only of one's behaviour but also of the behaviour of the society in which we live and which so often, by our silence, we endorse.

Restoration

In the Old Testament community of Israel those whom the world pushed to the margins of society were made central to God's purposes. Similarly, the kingdom of God is good news for the poor now, and not just in the life of the world to come. Those who are seen by the Pharisees as outside the kingdom, such as Zaccheus, were seen by Jesus to be at the centre of God's purposes in the world. They are restored to community, to health, to sanity and to loving relationships. Graham Cray comments,

> The sick are given back the possibility of an active role in society, the demonised are set free and restored to normal relationships, cleansed lepers can come back into the community. Those experiencing untimely bereavement have their loved ones and breadwinners restored. Jesus' table fellowship of tax collectors and sinners was the foretaste of their place in the Messianic banquet on the last day. His acceptance of women and little children gave them a special or best part in the Kingdom both present and future.[6]

The community which Jesus created had at its heart a need for the love of God as its motivating power in order to continue in existence. We have already seen how easy it is for people to interpret the Christian life as loving those who are able to love us back. But the point of the kingdom parables such as that of the banquet, and of the beatitudes, is to show that we are to love those who cannot possibly return such love in material terms. Each of us loves those who will love us in return, but we demonstrate our own fallenness when we shun those whom we dislike or who are different from us. Such relationships depend on 'the love of God being shed abroad in our heart'.

The church and the kingdom

The relationship of the church to the kingdom is therefore vital. The church is the only visible sign of the presence of the kingdom in the period between the first and second comings of Christ. With the eye of faith the church is so to pattern the kingdom in its behaviour that it becomes visible evidence of the existence of an alternative way of life in the midst of a dark world. It should be possible to look at the relationships, behaviour and stance of the church and see in them the pattern of the kingdom of God. Our problem is that many people who are impressed by Jesus Christ remain unimpressed by the behaviour of the church which bears his name.

The fact that the church is the link between the 'already' and the 'not yet' of the kingdom means that some aspects of the kingdom are present and some are future. Similarly, the kingdom is both 'like' and 'unlike' the church. Graham Cray comments that this has three implications:

> Firstly, a Kingdom that can be compared to aspects of ordinary life can be lived out in this life. Secondly the frequent 'twist in the tale' of the parables shows that the Kingdom is 'unlike' the way we are accustomed to live. The general tendency of parables is to confound our conventional and comfortable view. Thirdly, the Kingdom may not be precisely identified with human systems, concerns or aspirations. It is 'like' rather than 'the same as'.[7]

It is when Christians engaged in social action are criticized as being 'mere social workers' that the presence of the kingdom in the church comes to be of prime importance. Christians are not copying Jesus' acts of compassion using the same secular tools as everybody else to bring about secular ends. They are seeking to advance the mission of the kingdom in the power of the Spirit. That the justice and the power of the kingdom cannot be divorced from one another is often lost from sight both by those who engage in social action and by those who view the centre of the church's life as charismatic worship. Nor can either justice or power be divorced from the proclamation of the message of the kingdom.

But it is not only the power of the kingdom which the church is to represent. It is corporately to represent the 'upside-down values' of the kingdom. Jesus taught that the 'first shall be last and the last first'. Some non-Christians, knowing this, have asked why the people who hold office in the church are almost always drawn from those who have prestigious positions in the world. Why is it that barristers, solicitors and business people sit on our committees and lead our churches, when they are already so busy in their professional work that they have an ulcer or a rapidly deteriorating home life? At the same time many people who have taken early retirement or who are unemployed feel that they are of no use because they are hardly ever called upon to do anything! Surely something is radically wrong in this situation.

Others point to the way in which people dress up for church, seeing it as a social occasion. But this practice makes those who cannot afford such finery, uncomfortable. Worse, it may deter Christians from bringing friends to hear the gospel, since they would be embarrassed by such a display.

Even the cars in which we draw up to church, and the projects on which the church spends its money, can be barriers to the effectiveness of the church in representing the kingdom of God. If people cannot see us struggling to maintain a very different and distinctive life in our churches, how will they know that the kingdom of God is more than a myth?

The justice of the kingdom

The Old Testament prepares us for the justice of the kingdom by giving us a clear picture of God's own requirements for a king of Israel. Not only was the king to be fair in disputes but he was also to intervene when people could not secure justice for themselves. He was to champion the cause of those who were oppressed. Such a king reflected the character of God the King. The psalmist sings that, 'Righteousness and justice are the foundation of your throne.'[8]

Graham Cray points out that righteousness and justice form one quality not two. The cry of Amos, 'let justice roll on like a river, righteousness like a never failing stream!'[9] is a prayer for one event not two.[10]

When Gabriel came to Mary[11] he announced that Jesus would be given the throne of his father David and that he would reign over the house of Jacob for ever, his kingdom having no end. Mary's response to this in the Magnificat is to show that she understands the implications of giving birth to a king in the line of David.

> He has brought down the rulers from their thrones
>   but has lifted up the humble.
> He has filled the hungry with good things
>   but has sent the rich away empty.[12]

Jesus lived among the poor and many of his stories were most readily understandable by the poor. The story of the lost coin or the patched garment had emotive impact precisely because they captured some of the daily frustrations of those in the crowd whom Jesus saw as 'harassed and helpless, like sheep without a shepherd'. Not only were Jesus' miracles of sustenance (such as the feeding of the 5,000) about justice, but his healings too were about justice. People needed not only to be liberated from the oppressive social stigmas perpetrated by the religious authorities but to be restored to community from the structural evil of disease.

Jesus' Kingship extends over both natural and social evil and his lifting up of those whose lives have been hurt in either way restores them to the kind of life which he, the Creator, intended. Again we see that the power of God, the love of God and the compassion behind social action cannot be separated.

> If the agenda of the Kingdom can be defined from one perspective as the restoration of justice, the dynamic of the Kingdom is found in the ministry of the Holy Spirit.[13]

Jesus brings liberation not only to those who are physically behind bars or in debt or in bondage to cruel masters but also to those who need liberation from sin. He comes not only to feed the hungry but to offer them the bread of life which is his word. He brings sight to the physically blind and the spiritually blind. There is no aspect of life which is left untouched by the invasion of the power and the perspective of the kingdom.

The Holy Spirit cannot therefore be restricted to the worship of the church. When we attend conferences or read books on the Holy Spirit we often assume that the theme will be 'the charismatic gifts' and that the speaker or writer will be 'a charismatic'. But just as Christ's Lordship extends over all of life, so the Holy Spirit's mission is not just to bring his words (as conservative evangelicals emphasize) nor his gifts (as charismatics emphasize), but to rekindle the totality of Christ's mission and life in the church. The gap between 'charismatics' and social activists which so sadly exists today would be reduced if we could see a fuller picture of the work of the Holy Spirit in social and political action.

In effect, we have returned to the idea of the 'domain of control' to which we have already referred. Because we have divided life into the material and the spiritual, the sacred and the secular, the private and the public, the inner and the outer, we have created for ourselves a domain in which we have control and where we see no need for anything more than God's blessing on our actions. This realm of cause and effect does not seem to have any supernatural elements.

We find it almost impossible to see how ladling out soup to the homeless or distributing food parcels to the hungry or going to court with someone in debt needs the same degree of spiritual enabling as evangelism or any other overtly 'spiritual' pursuit. Because of this attitude those whose lives are given to social action on behalf of the poor are often accused of having lost their first love. It is assumed that their work requires no more spiritual resources than that of the Marxist or the humanist.

But if we believe that God does nothing apart from prayer and that the kingdom of God can be advanced only by the Spirit of God, then those who would be social activists must also be men and women of prayer dedicated to working in the Spirit. We shall have more to say about prayer and social justice in chapter eleven.

Evangelism

It is not, however, only the social activist who has much to learn from the pattern and power of the kingdom of God. The evangelist cannot assume that just because what he is doing is called 'evangelism', it is automatically sanctioned by Scripture. As Stephen Mott points out, evangelism is an important path to justice. Its goal is not just 'conversion' but the transformation of the individual into the person of Christ. The good news that the evangelist preaches is the good news of God's reign.

All too often in Western society people respond to the message of the evangelist by adding a new, religious 'compartment' to the rest of their life. But transformation is about an entire redirection of one's life, a new allegiance which brings an entirely new set of values.

The break which comes with the interest and the values of the world will be accomplished by a heightened awareness of moral responsibility. Paul states that Christian people become 'a new creation'. The radical message of Christianity will have social dimensions in that it will directly challenge structural evil as enshrined in unjust legislation and oppressive practices. But we must not underestimate the social implications which come from the transformed lives of the individuals. All too often we separate these two dimensions. One side claims that it is more important to 'save' people and then see a Christian society result. The other side points out that while evil institutions persist, oppression and poverty will also endure.

But in the gospels Zaccheus the tax collector provides a striking example of spiritual transformation. He responds with joy to Jesus and decides to redistribute his wealth to the poor and pay back those he had cheated. Jesus comments, 'today, salvation has come to this house'.[14] Frequently evangelistic revivals have gone hand in hand with social reform and such an integrated vision can be seen in the lives of past heroes such as Charles Finney or John Wesley. Would slavery ever have been abolished without the rise of the evangelical movement with its passion for Scripture?

Even Marxists such as Erich Fromm see the need for a transformed heart. He sees a dangerous error in Marx's

> . . . neglect of the moral factor in man. Just because he assumed that all the goodness of man would assert itself automatically when the economic changes had been achieved, he did not see that a better society could not be brought into life by people who had not undergone a moral change within themselves. He paid no attention, at least not explicitly, to the necessity of a new moral orientation, without which all political and economic changes are futile.[15]

Evangelism therefore points to the transcendence of God and his ability in the power of the Spirit to change completely the life of the individual. Without this emphasis on the power of the atonement in the life of the individual, social action is seen as icing on the cake.

People who see the transformation of the individual as both necessary and sufficient for the transformation of society fail to appreciate the extent to which a fallen society influences and shapes individuals. It is important to work at both the personal and the social levels at the same time if 'righteousness and justice' are to become more evident. The fact is that evangelism and social action are interdependent. Indeed one is impeded when the other is absent.

> It is time for evangelicals to refuse to use sentences that begin with 'the primary task of the Church is . . .' regardless of whether the sentence ends with evangelism or Bible teaching or social concern. They are all integral, necessary aspects of the Church's task.[16]

The question we need to ask is: 'What is the context in which we are seeking to bring the kingdom of God to these particular people?' It may be more appropriate at one point to feed people than to talk, whereas at other points people will need the challenge of the gospel message. But because Jesus is Lord of all and because the message of the whole church is to the whole person, we must both proclaim and demonstrate the good news of the kingdom of God.

We must not reduce the mission of the kingdom to either evangelism or social action. When we rediscover the priority of the kingdom of God in the life of the church we shall rediscover the unity which is necessary if Christ is going to build his church.

CHAPTER TEN

NEW LIFE, OLD LIFESTYLE?

To me the style is just the outside of content, and content the inside of style, like the outside and the inside of the human body. Both go together, they cannot be separated.

JEAN-LUC GODDARD

You don't have to signal a social conscience by looking a frump. Lace knickers won't hasten the holocaust. You can ban the bomb in a feather boa just as well as without, and a mild interest in the length of hemlines doesn't really disqualify you from reading Das Kapital *and agreeing with every word.*

JILL TWEEDIE

Envy in our time is confined to the contemplation of others of nearly equal income.

J. K. GALBRAITH

If you want to make a Christian feel guilty, it is no longer necessary to preach hell fire and damnation from the pulpit. All you need to do is to creep up behind an unsuspecting person and whisper the word 'lifestyle' in his ear. I guarantee that the result will be spectacular. The victim pales as he prepares to justify his standard of living in the light of his Christianity.

Perhaps I exaggerate a little. But it is no wonder that many Christians are confused and guilty about their lifestyle when they do not know whether affluence is a blessing from God or a barrier to effective Christian witness. As our standard of living has risen the division between Christians on this vital issue has grown.

There are two very distinct camps. The first draws attention to a direct link between Christian affluence and the decline of effective Christian witness in the West. The only remedy which they offer is the adoption of a simple lifestyle out of obedience to the gospel, compassion for the poor and responsibility towards the environment. The second group also points to a direct link between affluence and Christian witness. But this time an affluent Christian lifestyle is seen as evidence of the blessing of God. This has come to be called 'prosperity doctrine'.

Kenneth Hagin in his many booklets, such as *How God Taught Me about Prosperity*,[1] teaches us that God's will for all Christians is that they should be prosperous, healthy and a success in life. If they are not, this is due to a lack of faith on their part which he is only too happy to help them rectify. His message is very dependent on taking verses from the Bible such as Luke 6:38 and Psalm 34:10 and then using them to imply that those who are poor are personally responsible for their poverty which could be avoided if only they had more faith. Hagin also says that in order to love other people one must first be a 'success' oneself. He ends up in one passage by saying:

> Jesus Christ said that if we'd get into the word, we could have success in our lives now . . . The word says that I am to first love myself and then I can love my neighbour. I want myself to eat good, dress good, feel good, and have the best there is. If I love myself this way, I'll love others this way.[2]

Such teaching can appear to be common sense to those people who wish their lifestyle to be undisturbed by their Christianity. It will also appeal to narcissists who believe everything must focus on them. At first sight it may even appear reasonable that a God who loves us should wish us to have the best in life.

The problem comes when we reflect that God also wishes those who currently have nothing to have the best in life. We may be consuming resources which rightly belong to them. It is also questionable whether a person who is so highly motivated to get the best deal for himself will be as highly motivated in pursuing justice for the poor.

Lifestyle: a message to the world

The biblical statement that 'a man's life does not consist in the abundance of his possessions'[3] has two lessons to teach us. Firstly, it warns all those who desire wealth that it is possible to become extremely rich, enjoying every comfort which modern society could provide, and yet still live an impoverished life. Secondly, it warns those who would assess another person's life by purely material values. To do this is to accept that material possessions are the most important indicator of the nature of human life. It is therefore the height of irony that those who wish to combat materialism within Christianity usually do so by perpetuating its myth.

The word 'lifestyle' came into vogue in the 1970s along with Habitat and health food. Neil Simon's play *California Suite* contains one scene in which a woman, criticized for her comfortable lifestyle, protests, 'I don't have a lifestyle, I have a life.' Like it or not, our lifestyle is the shop window of our lives; the place where we publicly display our priorities for everyone to see. As Goddard says in a previous quote, style and content cannot be separated. Jesus said 'Let your light shine before men, that they may see your good deeds and praise your Father in heaven.'[4]

This does not mean that Christians should not have consumer goods. The important thing is the message we send to others by the way we use these goods. Two families can have the same number and quality of goods and the same type of home but send completely different messages to the rest of the community about their priority in life. When one walks into one home one feels temporarily its centre, such is the warmth of their hospitality. In a similar home, one might sit on the edge of one's seat trying not to spill any coffee lest dire consequences result. In such a home the carpet is of more value than the visitor. The question is not whether owning X or Y is wrong or not. It is what message we convey with our possessions.

Needs and wants

In his very helpful book *All You Love is Need*, sociologist, Tony Walter points out that we have a subtle attitude to our own possessions, even if we are fairly overt in our criticism of others. We accuse others of being greedy or selfish in their craving for luxury goods but justify our own purchase as meeting a *need*, not satisfying *greed*. Before we spend money we justify the imminent purchase by saying that we really do *need* it. Walter points out that many of these purchases are on behalf of others. We buy clothes and school equipment for our children, not out of a sense of greed but of *their need*.

We do not see this as 'greedy materialism', but as part of the responsibility of parenthood. Similarly within the household economy we may buy goods for each other and may spend only a relatively small amount on ourselves. Our purchases are therefore motivated by our perception of the needs of others and love for them. If this is so then calls for restraint in consumer spending may fall on deaf ears as we do not see ourselves as consumers for selfish reasons. Such a call

> . . . is asking individuals to spend less on others, which means a husband failing in his duty as breadwinner for his family, or it means a working mother failing to provide adequately for her children. Far from a worthy sacrifice, this is seen by the worker as immoral.[5]

So anybody writing about the morality of lifestyle, therefore, faces the problem that the majority of people do not see their way of life as either 'moral' or 'immoral' but as a necessity.

> Yet need is not ethically neutral, and part of us knows that too. If the children need new shoes, then they must have them. Need is not just a statement of fact, it also provides an imperative. It justifies the purchase. It is *good* reason, a very good reason.[6]

Once we have convinced ourselves that this is true, both morality and guilt drop away leaving us with a brand new set of justifications for our behaviour. Walter points out that although we dream of being able to afford 'a few little luxuries' at some time in the future when income allows, by the time we get to purchasing them, they have become needs.

> The notion that once we have met our basic needs, we may then move into the realm of luxuries is a lie, just as it is a lie to suppose that once a person's basic emotional and psychological needs have been met he may then begin to act in freedom. Once people enter the prison of needs they are never released.[7]

Here is a model of need as an addiction which is just as strong as heroin addiction. We can see that our prospective purchase will enable us to meet a particular desire but it is the desire which comes first and the purchase second. Some people even experience a let-down when they eventually possess the goods. Their sense of anticipation has been so strong that no product could fulfil their expectations. In such cases we are driven to formulate still further fantasies of who or what we could become if only we could have a particular product. It is this cycle of fantasy and dissatisfaction which advertising both depends on and stimulates by showing us pictures which represent our fantasies and then associating the product with them.

Three times in the first chapter of Romans (verses 24, 26, 28) Paul remarks of a society in decline that 'God gave them over . . .' The society was chasing freedom from God, but instead found judgment from God in that he allowed them to be governed by what they desired. This principle is true not only of the grossest forms of human sinfulness. It is also true when we express our satisfaction with 'normality' by a lifestyle which we describe as merely 'comfortable' rather than ostentatious.[8] If we are not careful we will find ourselves 'given over' to mediocrity.

The discipline of simplicity

Richard Foster is most helpful in pointing out that the external lifestyle is evidence of the inward reality of the Christian discipline of simplicity. Both are essential. It is impossible to attempt to change one's lifestyle without having first changed one's attitude to the world. Nor can those who are on an inward pilgrimage think that they can discover the freedom of simplicity as a discipline without it being seen in their lifestyle.

> Because we lack a divine centre our need for security has led us into an insane attachment to things. We must clearly understand that the lust for affluence in contemporary society is psychotic. It is psychotic because it has completely lost touch with reality. We crave things we neither need nor enjoy. We buy things we do not want, to impress people we do not like . . . The mass media has convinced us that to be out of step with fashion is to be out of step with reality. It is time we awaken to the fact that conformity to a sick society is to be sick. Until we see how unbalanced our culture has become at this point we will not be able to deal with the mammon spirit within ourselves nor will we desire Christian simplicity.[9]

Christians should beware the internal promptings of 'need' for, as we have already seen, it does not constitute a moral imperative.

We should learn from our experience that material products cannot satisfy a spiritual longing. A lonely person may express her loneliness in eating food and will convince herself that what she needs is a good meal when what she really wants is a good friend. A family living in a well-to-do neighbourhood may convince themselves that they need to replace most of their furniture and redecorate their house when what they really want is to be accepted by their neighbours as friends. I may convince myself that because I have been promoted I need a new car when what I really want is a new sense of authority to go with my position about which I am currently feeling insecure. Perhaps we would consume less if we were more honest about why we were buying things and if we could recognize afresh that the liberation which comes from material contentment is rooted in the knowledge that much that we crave is to be found in God alone.

Materialism and the Christian life

Some people are spoilt for choice while others are spoilt by lack of choice. The rich have power over their own lives and material destiny while the poor are powerless in material terms and have to accept what life offers them. Those who have poverty thrust upon them can be among the most materialistic, longing for those things which are beyond their grasp. For those of us who are comfortably off the way we live is an extremely personal expression of who we are, as we have the freedom to choose, and it is for this reason that we so quickly feel threatened if someone criticizes what we possess. We are always nervously looking over our shoulder at what the other person is doing, trying to assess what is acceptable and what is regarded as excessive.

But there is a sense in which the plans Jesus has for others are no concern of ours. As he said to Peter, who was curious to know what the future held for John (the 'beloved disciple'), 'What is that to you? You must follow me.'[10] God calls us to work out our discipleship before him as our first priority. Nevertheless, we insist on deriving our status and self-worth from a comparison with those around us. If this were not true there would be an objective standard of consumption by which we could all be judged. Yet when someone tells us that we would increase our Christian integrity by buying a cheaper car or moving into a smaller house we feel that our personal territory has been invaded.

One of the major problems with Christian discussion of lifestyle is its negative cast. Yet Jesus said, 'The thief comes only to steal and kill and destroy; I have come that they may have life and have it to the full.'[11] Tom Sine says in *The Mustard Seed Conspiracy*:

> So much of the literature on the simplification of lifestyles seems to be only about 'cutting back and giving up' a chunk of the 'good life', and I want to holler 'wait a minute – whoever said that the rat race we are caught up with has anything to do with the good life?'[12]

What we need is to redefine the 'good life' from a biblical perspective, learning to celebrate life more while consuming less. There is a tension here between the *aesthetic* and the *ascetic*. The 'Christian mind' approach to the world requires us to become deeply involved in our culture. As Christians we should be involved in the arts, sciences and politics and should enjoy life to the full, showing that this world was created by a good God for us to enjoy. We should use our leisure time to the full, pursue hobbies and bring up our children with a real appreciation of music, theatre and literature. Our homes can still be beautiful, after all there is a great deal of difference between luxury and 'stylishness'. You cannot buy the latter.

All this is world-affirming; a celebration of life. Living as Christians does not mean becoming recluses or ascetics but it does mean that we must see our gifts and resources as coming from and belonging to God. All that we have and all that we stand for is to be a joyful celebration of him. This is part of the freedom to live the 'abundant life' which Christ brings.

Yet the Bible is unequivocal on the relationship between materialism and spirituality. Firstly, materialism makes it impossible to listen to and heed the whole gospel. Ezekiel experienced this as a prophet called by God. The people came to hear what the Lord had to say to them through his ministry but their attitude to the message was such that they could not possibly put it into practice. God says about them,

> 'My people crowd in to hear what you have to say, but they don't do what you tell them to do. They treat your words as simple songs and continue their greedy ways. To them you are nothing more than an entertainer singing love songs or playing a harp.'[13]

One of the tell-tale signs that materialism has infiltrated the church is when preaching has ceased to be prophetic and has become mere entertainment. We comment on the quality of the preaching over the Sunday lunch rather than wrestle with the implications of obedience to the word of God. It also becomes difficult to preach the whole gospel because parts of it are so pointed that they become an embarrassment.

Secondly, materialism changes the criteria by which we assess the fruits of Christian discipleship. We become satisfied with the fact that people are pleasant to us and don't appear to 'rock the boat' and we confuse this with their being Christian. It is sometimes said of Christians that they believe in 'faith, hope and niceness, and the greatest of these is niceness'. Jesus told us that 'even the Gentiles' are nice to one another, inviting one another to dinner, and caring for each other. He called us to love our enemies; a completely different ball game.

The residue of biblical Christianity which materialism leaves behind provides us with sufficient spiritual veneer to be able to live our Christian lives if nothing disturbs us. But when somebody lashes out at a person who has no spiritual resources or roots he or she often lashes back. What and who we are is most evident not when everything is going well but when it is going badly. It is then that the source of our security is plain for everyone to see.

Materialism does not allow us to put Christianity first. It will allow us to put it second. But as Jesus said, 'you cannot serve God and money'. Second place means last place. Richard Foster has commented on this, saying that if we do not seek the kingdom of God first we do not seek it at all.

Thirdly, a church which is riddled with materialism cannot confront those powers and institutions in our society which are generating it. The idolatry of technological progress, the evils of poverty and the retreat into private comfort remain largely unchallenged if the church which is called to be a prophetic and distinctive community in the world is not distinguishable from it. The more we absorb the world's values, the less we are able to challenge its very nature. How distinctive are we? That is the question.

The security of riches

The claim that material possessions provide security is a myth. The rich have as many problems arising out of their humanness as the poor. If they were mere animals then they would lack for nothing, but men and women are 'living souls'. We must not perpetuate the myth of riches by pretending that wealth makes people superior. Their needs are exactly the same as those of the poor. It is for this reason that it is so hard for the rich to enter the kingdom of God. The life of the kingdom is available only to those who live by its values, worship the King and draw on its life. But materialism offers the rich person another kingdom with the opposite values, with self as king and with no need for any spiritual life. It provides its followers with such tangible security that they cannot see the need for the care of an invisible heavenly Father. 'How hard it is for a rich man to enter the kingdom of heaven.' How right Jesus was.[14]

Materialism, far from creating a society characterized by security and joyful celebration, creates *anxiety*. Adverts promise us that the fruit of our riches will make us the people we long to be: suave and macho or feminine and sultry. The fat will become thin, the shy confident, and the ugly beautiful. But when we look in the mirror, exhausted from running the rat race, we see anxious faces. Materialism is always trying to change us into people more acceptable to others.

God accepts us as we are with all our imperfections. That is the basis for true liberation. Poverty is no blessing in itself for it is a denial of the adequacy of God's provision and when perpetuated by injustice, is an insult to God. But neither are riches a blessing as modern-day 'prosperity doctrine' would have it. The writer of Proverbs sums it up beautifully by saying:

> Give me neither poverty nor riches,
> but give me only my daily bread.
> Otherwise, I may have too much and
> disown you
> and say, 'Who is the LORD?'
> Or I may become poor and steal,
> and so dishonour the name of my God.[15]

He also comments,

> Wealth is worthless in the day of wrath,
> but righteousness delivers from death.[16]

The parallel here is not between riches and poverty but between riches and righteousness. For those who cling desperately to this life for security, the next life offers no hope. Only those who can see this world as a gift from God and live in it in that light can fully enter into the life of the next. Our style of life is intimately related to our view of death. Is it an end of all we love? Or an entrance into all we have longed for?

Dealing with guilt

Materialism leads to guilt which in turn breeds inertia. Many Christians seem to think that guilt is natural and acceptable, but Christ died to liberate us from all oppression, including that of guilt. The liberation which he brings leads us to act rather than to become introspective. Guilt petrifies and stultifies our Christian faith. Like all idols materialism cannot deliver the goods. Jesus says, 'Do not be anxious about tomorrow', so why are so many anxious? He says, 'Your heavenly Father knows you need these things', so why are so many insecure? Nowhere in the Scriptures are we told to feel guilty.

The general *feeling* of guilt which pervades many Western Christians is foreign to Scripture. The Bible tells us that we *are* guilty before God, but it also tells us of the provision Christ has made for us on the cross. What it does tell us to do is repent. The difference is that the guilty person dwells on her sin and is unable to act; the repentant person dwells on the demands of a holy God and is liberated by her repentance.

So many Christians have been made to feel guilty when the subject of Christian lifestyle is raised, and it has been completely unnecessary. If they have committed a sin then God waits eagerly for their repentance and renewed determination to live effectively for him. If they have not sinned why do they feel guilty?

> Nowhere do the scriptures command us to *feel* guilty. They only declare that we *are* guilty. This declaration that we have fallen short of God's expectations is a legal description of our relationship with God. A right relationship with God is not restored through a feeling of guilt; nor is habitual behaviour overcome through a heroic and independent effort of sheer willpower. Restoration with God comes through the grace of God. The legwork on our part is to say 'yes' to the divine 'yes'.[17]

One of the easiest ways to produce guilt is to compare ourselves with those who are living below the subsistence level. Yet the very fact that we can choose to give up possessions is the first dissimilarity between us and them. We cannot begin to approach their level of material poverty. The question is not 'How can I identify materially with the poorest of the earth?' but 'How can I live appropriately in the light of their existence?'

Are comparisons odious?

The pictures of famine in sub-Saharan Africa and the statistics which flow constantly from the news media describe a human tragedy of immense proportions. Yet although such a tragedy can motivate television viewers to give generously on one occasion it seems unable to motivate us consistently to live a different life in the light of it. The fact is that people respond not to statistics but within relationships. The enormity of the world's tragedies is as likely to lead to a sense of powerlessness and paralysis as it is to action. Large amounts of information soon begin to wash over us like waves and people find it difficult to 'think globally and act locally' as the modern proverb requires of them.

In fact, in our daily lives we compare ourselves not with those in the Third World, but with those living around us. The more those living around us are like us, the more secure we will feel in our chosen lifestyle. Robert Franks in his book *Choosing the Right Pond* says,

> . . . our needs depend very strongly on the identities of those with whom we choose to associate closely. When we associate with people of modest means, the things we feel we need are more modest than when we associate with people of greater means . . . someone who is tired of feeling bad about the kind of house she lives in can start to feel good about that same house by simply switching to a less wealthy circle of friends. She can play in a different league.[18]

H. L. Mencken put this beautifully when he defined wealth as any income that is at least $100 more per year than the income of one's wife's sister's husband.[19] In defining the things we think we need it really matters with which group of people we compare ourselves. This is largely dictated by the area in which we live. It does not matter to me whether Rockerfeller earns a million dollars a year more, but it may worry me if my neighbour begins to earn £2,000 a year more than me. If I earn £10,000 in a neighbourhood where most are on £15,000 a year I will feel poor and under pressure. However, if I earn £10,000 a year in a neighbourhood where most people are on £6,000 or less or where there is high unemployment, then although I may be materially comfortable I will feel a little 'uncomfortable' at times.

Local status is therefore extremely important. We do not wish to 'keep up with the Joneses'. To do so would be too overt and vulgar. It is enough to be thought not *inferior* to the Joneses. It is therefore extremely important where Christians choose to live and for what reason. People move houses for an enormous number of reasons both good and bad. Some of the reasons are 'below the surface' such as when a family moves house because of promotion, which could lead them to wish to live among a different (superior) group of people.

Few people think of moving house in terms of calling. Yet this is what God asks us to do. Where is God asking us to live? The decision must be taken very carefully.

Voluntary simplicity

The Bible recognizes that I have rights to property which are part of my enjoyment of God's creation and of the fruit of my labour. Such an assumption forms the background to the awful story of Ananias and Sapphira in Acts 4. Christianity does not coerce us to give up our possessions and therefore voluntary simplicity is the only form which Scripture will accept. This is one of the reasons why a change of lifestyle induced by guilt is unacceptable; guilt is coercive and has only temporary effects. It is the 'cheerful' giver whom the Lord loves.

Self-forgetful simplicity is not self-denying but life-affirming. It calls into question the massive economic forces marshalled against us by an economic system which has idolized progress and material welfare. Schumacher writes,

> What is the great bulk of advertising other than the stimulation of greed, envy and avarice? It cannot be denied that industrialism, certainly in its capitalist form, openly employs these human failings – at least three of the seven deadly sins – as its motive force.[20]

As economist Richard Layard puts it,

> In a poor society a man proves to his wife that he loves her by giving her a rose, but in a rich society he must give her a dozen roses.[21]

Where does this chapter leave us? It does not give us any easy answers, and that for a good reason. We are called to struggle in combat with the world's values, 'working out our salvation' until we go to be with the Lord. No objective standard can be drawn up as to what constitutes an acceptable Christian lifestyle. This would imply a new legalism, a new bondage.

There is no merit in trying to induce guilt in order to get people to own fewer possessions. This is not the problem and never will be the problem. *It is the lack of security and confidence in God which is the real issue.* Modern Christians find it almost intolerably difficult to bypass the seemingly obvious security of the material world for the possible risks of a life lived by faith in an invisible God. Goddard's words at the beginning of this chapter tell us that style and content are inextricably intertwined. We have therefore returned to the most basic question at the heart of the Christian faith: What is it that we believe, and how can we show the world that it is true?

One Nigerian student commented on the state of the Western church, 'You have found a way peacefully to co-exist with the world.' This is too high a price to pay for something which death will strip from us before we are ushered into the presence of God.

CHAPTER ELEVEN

PRAYER AND SOCIAL JUSTICE

The work of praying is prerequisite to all other work in the kingdom of God, for the simple reason that it is by prayer that we couple the powers of heaven to our helplessness . . .

OLE HALLESBY

The most odious of concealed narcissisms – prayer.

JOHN FOWLES

Prayer is one of those activities which lies at the heart of Christian discipleship, yet which few of us understand. Many of us find prayer one of the hardest aspects of Christian discipleship. Some struggle on with it while, undoubtedly, others attempt to live their Christian life without it.

Those who are heavily committed to social action are often assumed to have devoted their energies to it at the expense of prayer and worship. They are caricatured as regarding the material needs of the world as more important than spiritual discipline or the eternal destiny of the individual. This criticism should be groundless, for, as we shall see in this chapter, those who are immersed in social action should also be those who are most committed to a life of prayer.

There was a tendency in the 1970s for prayer to become centred less and less on social and global issues and more on personal needs and church programmes. Richard Lovelace in his *Dynamics of*

Spiritual Life writes of the prayer life of American churches in the 1970s as inherently passive and socially conservative because it always focused on 'spiritual' considerations (the search for meaning, inner emotional satisfaction), rather than on a realistic effort to meet the real problems in society.[1]

Yet those who are passionately concerned about social issues must face the question of the relationship between prayer and social justice. How does one pray about the catastrophe in sub-Saharan Africa or about unemployment?

I recently faced the question personally when watching the news on television. There was violence on the streets, children wasting away in Ethiopia, misery in the dole queues, and child abuse. Moved by this portrayal of the human condition, I attempted to pray. However, I found that words would not come. A deep sense of alienation stole over me and a sense of powerlessness took hold of me.

At first I was frustrated that I could not pray, but then light dawned. Was not this groaning on behalf of others in the presence of God, more prayer-like than some of my most articulate, fluent prayers? Did it not centre more on Christ's response to human need when on the cross?

Maybe the attempt to be always articulate in prayer sometimes actually hampers us from entering in to the feeling of others in prayer? My previous attempts to pray for those who feel utterly crushed and devastated, without myself identifying with what they were going through, suddenly seemed very superficial.

Articulate prayer

Of course, prayer is offered in many forms, among them contemplation, meditation, thanksgiving, praise and intercession. But in expressing these there seem to be two schools of thought.

The first, in which I was raised, sees prayer as articulation. It is a response to God's revelation of himself to us in articulate propositional truth. Because God has revealed himself to us in words we can understand, we express ourselves to him in this way. This school takes the many lucid prayers in the Scriptures, including those of our Lord himself, as models for our own prayer life. In praying for social issues this school has much to teach us.

Articulate prayer depends upon thorough analysis of the situation for which one is praying. Instead of conducting intellectual debate and expressing our views away from the presence of God, such prayer acknowledges that God is one with us in our deliberations, and that all decisions, whether technical or moral, are taken in the presence of God and can therefore be brought to him in prayer. In this kind of prayer we submit the realm of the intellect to God and acknowledge his Lordship.

In corporate prayer, informed leadership can clear the head, move the heart and bring God's people to an experience of unity which is the opposite of the violent polarization sometimes demonstrated in the world outside.

The mystery of prayer

Yet articulate prayer, though it has much to offer, is limited. There are times when we do not know how to pray, either because we do not know what 'the right and the good' is in a particular situation or because we are temporarily overwhelmed by the enormity of some aspect of it.

Evangelicals are beginning to find that valuable lessons about spirituality can be learned from other Christian traditions. Such traditions draw their strength from the incarnation and Christ's subsequent taking up into God of man's human experience. Prayer is based on the nature of God and its expression in Christ. Contemplation and meditation generate great insights into the problems of a troubled world not because the one who contemplates is necessarily caught up in the business of that world, but because Christ understands each aspect of humanity's predicament.

This point of view has formed one of the foundations of the mystical traditions over the last two thousand years. It has been expressed recently by Kenneth Leech in his books *True Spirituality* and *The Social God*, and also in a two-part essay entitled 'Solitude and Solidarity'.[2]

He states explicitly that he wishes 'to point to the need to see the renewal of Christian spirituality and Christian social prophecy as a unity.'[3] Again he states that 'contemplation is also necessary to social action if it not is to degenerate into mere reformism'.[4]

Christians must learn to be still before God. We shall thus learn the difference between God-ordained action, which there is always time to complete, and a false activism which expresses the tyranny of time. Only then shall we be still enough to 'listen to society'.[5]

This solitude is neither individualistic or isolationist but necessary if social action is to be God's work and not merely human. Both those who are searching for the social dimension of spirituality and those who are looking for the spiritual basis for social action will find great riches in this interaction between prayer and social justice.

Those sceptics who believe that immersion in the problems of social action leads us away from concern about spirituality have stood reality on its head. Immersion in the problems of this world leads us to seek new depths in prayer and a more concrete and robust spirituality. The quest for social justice is in effect the other side of the quest for true spirituality.

Richard Lovelace states that 'most Christians would probably agree that prayer has little to do with social justice'.[6] He also says that 'this is because most of those who are praying are not praying about social issues and most of those who are active in social issues are not praying very much'.[7] These Christians have misunderstood both prayer and social action.

Social action and grace

This misunderstanding is expressed by those who think that Christian social action is part of a 'religion of works'. Such people view evangelism as something 'spiritual' which can be accomplished only by God's grace, whereas social action is something which man does by himself. It is therefore a lesser priority, if in this view it is a priority at all. This view must be corrected. Social action is just as dependent on God's grace as evangelism. Grace frees us for love and action. We act in love, in response to God's gracious invitation to us:

> Christian social action, indeed all Christian conduct properly understood, is grounded in the grace of Jesus Christ. Because of sin we are dependent upon God's power through Christ working for us, in us and through us. Christian social action builds on everything that the Scriptures have to say about the Grace of God in salvation. As a form of Christian ethics, it starts with the Cross, with appropriation of atonement.[8]

All that is done in the name of Christ, then, must be immersed in prayer. Whether in the realm of politics, economics, social work or evangelism it is true that 'the weapons of our warfare are not worldly but have divine power to destroy strongholds' (2 Corinthians 10:4).

The value of prayer in the social realm is brought out in a telling example in Jane Hatfield's booklet *Creative Prayer*:

> Many who visit Mother Teresa and her Missionaries of Charity are surprised that every lunch time they leave their life sustaining work in dispensaries and in the home for the dying. Why go back so soon? To pray. *They have learnt that to work without prayer is to achieve only what is humanly possible, and their desire is to be involved in divine possibilities.*[9] (my emphasis)

Attitudes to power

Another problem, associated with our satisfaction with mere human possibilities, arises from our attitude to power. Our attitude to both prayer and social action is affected by our view of power. Prayer is rarely the resort of those who have been deceived by the powers of this age. Those who feel threatened by such power find it so tangible that prayer seems too fragile as a weapon against it. For them powerlessness also means hopelessness, a false equation.

Similarly, those who wield secular power are tempted to dismiss prayer, for they can apparently change much without its aid. They may also be reluctant to challenge the *status quo* which gave them their power. Those who are convinced of the hopelessness of a situation will not subscribe to action either, since it will always be token action as far as they are concerned. Those who wield power and who *do* take action are tempted to attribute its success to their own power rather than to God's grace.

The Christian must learn the lesson from Jesus that although one may possess little in the way of solutions, that little can become much more in God's hands. When faced with five thousand hungry men, plus women and children, Jesus took a little food, blessed it, broke it and distributed it. What further encouragement do we need to fuse the little we have to offer a needy world with a deeper commitment to prayer?

The idolatry of results

One of the problems, then, is that we think we can solve the problems of the world by our own power. Ironically, another is that we attempt to tie *God* down to solving our problems for us. Some people view lack of 'answers' to prayer (by which they mean 'yes' answers) as a fundamental obstacle to faith. Yet the object of prayer is not pragmatic problem-solving (though God frequently does 'answer' prayer), but being with a God in whom we delight.

Modern people who delight in the 'cause and effect' which they have come to expect from science are disappointed with a supposedly important aspect of religion which delivers the goods somewhat erratically. As Jacques Ellul has pointed out, in a society which is dedicated to 'doing' and to 'efficiency', prayer appears both unrealistic and unpractical.

> The problem now is that we find ourselves a part of this competition for doing, for prayer has long been understood as a means of attaining results. Doubtless this tendency has its roots in the Bible. Prayer is presented to us as having power over everything over which God has power, over demons, over sickness, over other people, over nature. It is a way of acting upon God, and over everything through him. It is power. Remember the episode of the withered fig tree. With that beginning, by reduction, rationalising and individualising we have now come up with a power *of* prayer. We no longer seek through prayer, a conformity with God's will, which makes our speech more true, hence efficacious. We seek rather to achieve direct results without bothering about the truth or the special will of God, or with our own obedience.[10]

If Ellul is right, there is a great difference between 'mountain-moving prayer' understood as an attitude of faith, and 'mountain-moving prayer' which is simply a hunger for tangible results. This latter kind of prayer does not surround everything we do, only those things which we cannot accomplish on our own. As technology makes us more powerful, the need for prayer seems to diminish. As welfare grows so the need for God to be involved in social action diminishes.

This attitude is most prevalent in contemporary attitudes to healing. If a person recovers from an illness due to the skill of a doctor or effective drug therapy this is considered to belong to the realm of scientific endeavour. Little glory goes to God, even glory reflected from the physician's God-given skill. The recovery is due to a process of cause and effect which is explained scientifically. There seems to be no place in the picture for God.

As human knowledge and expertise grow, the area of the *miraculous* diminishes because the domain of the miraculous has come to apply only to that area which man cannot explain and control. At the same time, however, those incidents described as miraculous become more and more spectacular – not necessarily because God is performing more miracles but because *we are now blind* to the thousands of times when God answers prayer through the expertise of the doctor, given by God in the first place.

We will accept as miraculous only those occurrences of healing which interrupt the chain of cause and effect and which are therefore the most spectacular. If even our attitude to healing (which most Christians regard as a legitimate matter for prayer) is so impoverished, it is no surprise that the world of economics is so totally dominated by secular and mechanistic thinking.

Economics is a complete mystery to many people, including economists. But we have been convinced of its power even though we may not understand how this power operates. The problem is that the economic world-view has become a tyrant. Instead of serving people and their material needs it has come to serve its own abstract ends which are ideologically determined.

Under capitalism (whose tenets are the inevitability of progress, the acceptability of self-interest, and the 'regrettable' but necessary existence of poverty and inequality), men and women are subservient to the demands of 'the system'. We understand how to pray for *people*, but because economics has generated a self-contained system of explanation, many issues which should drive us to our knees in prayer seem to be the responsibility of 'the system' rather than of the church. Yet again we have been seduced by the secular point of view and have therefore lost the power to pray effectively over economic issues, since when we do so we believe ourselves to be encroaching on ground which rightly belongs to others.

The assumption that prayer takes over primarily when human ability and means are inadequate deals a death blow to prayer, for as we develop and assert ourselves, using the means provided by the technological society, the realm of prayer shrinks. However, the kind of prayer which looks to success as its creation is doomed and cannot be called true prayer.

One of the reasons why prayer for social justice is not 'popular' may be that it is difficult to tell whether one's prayer has been 'successful' when one is praying for something as apparently amorphous as social justice. It is more rewarding to pray for the specific problems of individuals, knowing that one's prayer has been answered if their problems disappear. One prays for social justice because one believes in prayer, whatever its rewards, and because one also longs for social justice.

Advocacy and identification

Our model of prayer comes from Christ who is our advocate before the Father. He pleads our cause because he understands the frailties of being human, having identified with us in every way through his incarnation and death. In him we find resolved our two forms of prayer. *The prayer of advocacy*, such as that of Jesus in John 17, is the prayer on behalf of others. Abraham pleading for Sodom and Gomorrah or Moses pleading for Israel shows us that such prayer, though articulate in that one is presenting the case of others to God, can still be passionate. *The prayer of identification* seeks as Jesus did to stand where those who are suffering stand, to open ourselves to the possibilities of the Holy Spirit reproducing in us the same sense of alienation or frustration that they feel (*cf.* John 11:33, 35, 41–42).

This is the prayer of groans and tears; prayer as a tool used by God to strip aside more and more of the barriers we build between ourselves and those who suffer, until we share with them in their experience, through prayer. Sometimes, when faced with social crisis or injustice, looking for an 'answer' can be a means of *not* being involved in the same painful process oneself. It is possible to be pulled into the world's game of seeking satisfactory solutions to intellectual puzzles without personal risk or cost. One may find such a solution and still be powerless for a million reasons, for the world allows their implementation only by those in a recognized position of power.

There is, however, another way, for the person who commits himself to a life of advocacy on behalf of others and identifies with them through prayer becomes a part of God's answer. On this issue at least his life counts for much, for instead of looking dispassionately at the way in which the balances are tilting against the poor and the dispossessed, and then filing away some intellectual evaluation, he has jumped on the scales himself, willing to be counted in with them even though he may be very different, and edging the scales towards justice. Ironically, too, such a person, who is taken up only with what God wants to do rather than what he would like to see God do, will perceive God's faithful answers to prayer in ways and places to which the 'prayer pragmatist' is blind.

A call to prayer

As we shall see in the next chapter, on worship, one of the distinctive characteristics of a Christian quest for justice is a new kind of inwardness. Christians are not called to frenetic activity, nor are they called to be volunteer social workers. They are called to be like their Lord. It is impossible to divorce spirituality from social concern in the life of Jesus and the two should be as closely linked in both the corporate and individual expressions of the Christian faith.

If the fledgling movement among evangelicals to recover their social conscience, is to demonstrate the gospel to the world in the Spirit and in power, then it must recover a heart of prayer. Some of those involved in social action have rightly reacted to the privatized faith of some of our forebears. But those who would wear the mantle of Shaftesbury, Wilberforce and the Clapham Sect in the latter half of the twentieth century must also have their passion for prayer. Without such a passion for God, evangelical social concern will disappear as yet another brief reactionary 'fad' which achieved little for God.[11]

CHAPTER TWELVE

WORSHIPPING THE GOD OF JUSTICE

The best measure of a spiritual life is not its ecstasies, but its obedience.

OSWALD CHAMBERS

For the Christian, worship is the context of life. It is not just an activity which we engage in when we go to church on Sundays. All that we stand for and represent is dictated by the God whom we worship, for all worship involves an exchange. As we give ourselves to God in worship, he gives himself to us. It is important that we are fully open to him, struggling to worship all of God and not only those aspects of him that we find easy to comprehend.

Given the routines which the church has attached to regular worship, it is a constant temptation to think of God routinely too. There may be particular choruses or hymns which we feel have led us into a spirit of worship in the past, and we look to them to produce the same atmosphere of worship in every service. There may be passages of Scripture, gestures, ways of speaking, which become associated with an atmosphere of worship. It is a short step for the church, instead of expressing worship to God through such things unconsciously, to seek the atmosphere of worship by consciously concentrating on these things instead of on the person of God himself. In some services people do not feel that they have worshipped God unless they have raised their hands or unless there have been several messages in tongues. In other services it is the quality of the hymn-singing or the silent reverence for the words of the prayer book which represent an appropriate atmosphere.

These all show that we have many forms through which to worship God. Many of them are purely cultural expressions and will vary from country to country and from town to town.

Worship is a right which belongs, not to us, but to God because he is God. In worship we are in effect saying to God 'You alone are worthy.' That remains true whatever the quality of the experience of worship for those in the congregation. Yet many Christians behave as if worship were *their* right, and as if they had a right to a particular quality of experience of God every time they meet with him. But true worship is self-forgetful. It is not concerned with experience, it is being taken up with God. The person engaged in true worship says in effect, 'Whatever I feel or don't feel is up to you; all I have come to say is that you alone are worthy.' It is being wholly taken up with God which restores our perspective on ourselves and on the world.

Choosing God

Where 'self' has become more important than God himself, people may feel that they are quite within their rights in having favourite ways of approaching God and thinking of him although they would not express it in this way. As we saw in chapter two, this can easily lead to idolatry as people begin to worship a God they find easy to understand and easy to live with. Somebody who is living in adultery while professing faith as a Christian may say that he does not believe that God will judge him for doing so, since God is a God of love. Such people deliberately ignore a whole part of God's character, choosing to emphasize one aspect which, when stripped away from the totality of who God is, becomes mere sentiment.

Similarly, many people make their own judgment about what God is like, based on their own feelings. When faced with biblical passages such as those in which God commands Israel to go to war, or where Jesus talks of the reality of hell, they respond by saying that 'God is not like that'. Thus they make God in their own image. Worship cannot easily challenge them or stretch their thinking, because they are controlling their picture of God. He becomes no more than a puppet who will bless their behaviour as they pull the strings.

This is true not only for individuals but for the whole church. The church stands between the revelation of God in Scripture and the social and idolatrous pressures of the world. It is constantly in tension, because on the one hand it wishes to remain true to

Scripture and on the other hand it is under pressure to settle down with the world. Part of the way in which the modern church expresses this tension is evident in the relationship between worship and justice. The psalmist repeatedly praises God for his justice not only because he raises up the poor but also because his judgment is holy. This aspect of worship is almost entirely lacking in the modern church. Very few contemporary Christian hymn writers take up the themes of justice and judgment.

As we have seen in previous chapters the Christian passion for justice in society is derived not from political ideologies but from the doctrine of God. In practice the way in which this is reinforced in the life of the church is through worship as well as through Bible study and preaching. 'We become what we worship,' and if the people of God do not worship God for his justice they cannot become the community of justice. If social action is to be conducted in the power of the Spirit it must draw its vision for society and the strength to carry on in the face of adversity from a rich worship life. If that aspect of worship is absent, social action will be reduced to a rather shallow exercise which may at its worst have no more spiritual significance than any other humanitarian act.

But the relationship of God to his people in worship is a two-way relationship. It is as people with a passion for justice go out into the world and seek to make their society more pleasing to God that they find themselves hurt and broken by the amount of social evil they come up against. They need to come back together into the healing community of worship and cry out to God knowing he shares their concerns and their priorities. If the church is not articulating God's justice in its liturgy, and if it does not show that God identifies with even the smallest frustrations of the poor, those who are deeply involved in the lives of others and who need to be sustained themselves may well become cynical about the promise of abundant life to all who live for Christ in the world.

Those who are impoverished and oppressed need themselves to be able to come and express their heartfelt cry through the liturgy (whether formal or informal). In language which conveys something to them, they need to hear that God understands their situation and is in it with them, suffering with them. The expression of daily suffering, along with the language and the physical expression of joy, must be ever present in the life of the church. We need to give one another room to breathe and to express ourselves differently. A crowd of enthusiastic football supporters expresses its emotion differently from the more restrained enthusiasm of Wimbledon spectators.

It would be a mistake, however, to think that worship is important only as a refuelling stop which keeps us going from Monday to Saturday. The church is not just about mission. We should not feel guilty about gathering for worship, believing that we should always be dispersed into the world of work. Nor is the church fundamentally about sermons which prepare us to go back into the world of work. This kind of assumption is mistaken on two counts.

Firstly, it indicates that our concern is 'What did I get out of it?' – a question focusing on the self rather than on God. When our worship accurately reflects the God who has revealed himself in Scripture, and is not seen as an end in itself, we shall find the refreshment that we need, as a by-product.

Secondly, the idea of worship as a refuelling for the rest of the week capitulates to the view that life is really about the routine of work, from which we are allowed to 'take a break' from time to time. Rather, life should be seen as an expression of worship which provides the context for all that we do.[1] If the church succumbs to the view that worship is just a break from work, it is no wonder that people who have no taste for religious things will turn to sport or the Sunday papers for relaxation and entertainment. Because so many Christians have this model of worship at the back of their minds, they feel cheated when church worship turns out to be more boring than a cosy hour with the papers or tending the garden.

The concept of attending 'church worship' as a duty is doomed to failure from the outset. One cannot expect to focus on the world for six days and on God for a few hours on Sunday. God would appear alien and rituals of worship would be opaque. No, worship must be the order of every day, motivating especially those parts of our lives which we have hitherto cut off from the Creator's influence in order to exert personal control over them.

Work and worship

Because the Christian views life as a sacramental gift from God, there is a fundamental link between work and worship. For the secularist the meaning of life is found within the world itself as he or she perceives it. But for the Christian the presence of God in the whole of life means that there is no one place or time to worship God or to acknowledge his presence.

Worship can restore one's perspective on life as much in the boardroom or on the shopfloor as on our knees in the church. Whereas the world has become opaque to those without faith, those who perceive human history with the eye of faith recognize that Christ is bringing his purposes to completion even in the midst of much evil. Worship is, therefore, a way of seeing the world as well as the offering of ourselves to God. It is seeing all that happens in the light of God and his purposes. In fact worship is the very opposite of *the economic point of view* and is its corrective. Whereas economics deals only with observable events and behaviour, worship ascribes worth to somebody who cannot be seen on the basis of the finished work of the cross, an event which materially speaking was a failure. Worship looks behind the events of history for reasons which can be perceived only by those with faith. The whole of life is cast in a light which places the reign of God and his kingdom at centre stage. People who act according to its dictates and values will often find themselves doing things which are not only 'uneconomic' but which are patently absurd. Think of the waste of investment in training and human capital when a doctor or nurse, teacher or engineer becomes a missionary and goes to the Third World with her talent! Do we add up the loss to the economy? No, we rejoice in her obedience to the calling of God. As we have commented before, economics must be subject to the norms set by the concept of stewardship and to the values of the kingdom, enlivened by worship.

Remembrance

One of the most important aspects of worship for the Christian is remembrance. Israel erected stones at Gilgal to enable future generations to remember God's grace to them there. There are many places in the Old Testament where God calls Israel to remember what he had done for them in times past. In a busy world in which we are carried along by our routines and our full diaries it is difficult to stop and remember the goodness of God in our lives and be thankful. It is also difficult to stop and meditate on who God has revealed himself to be.

Here is an important role for the elderly in our churches. As they grow older God gives them a special gift; the memory of their early years sharpens. At the end of our lives God prepares us to put our house in order. He enables us to meditate and create a story out of our lives which makes sense of all the disparate events which have happened to us. Not only do elderly people want someone to listen to them as they tell their story, but we need to listen to them. The stories of the 'elders' which tell of God's graciousness in years gone by are the links which fuse generations together.

It is unfortunate that in our attitude to our elderly and to the whole ageing process, we show our own fear of getting old. We put our old people away or we treat them as if they have nothing left to offer. It is not so in many other cultures, where to be 'full of years' brings the greatest honour and a recognition of wisdom. Without a place in our worship-life for this story-telling, generations become discrete in their experience and each one reinvents the wheel. Many of us have no 'worship-history' and some even believe that the Holy Spirit started moving only in the last twenty-five years!

One of the ways in which God enabled Israel to remember was the Sabbath. God instituted his own rhythm into his creation so that people would work and rest and in their rest have time to regain their perspective. One of the hallmarks of the process of secularization in our society is the extent to which this rhythm of work and rest is denied. Whether it is through the pressure for Sunday trading or the seriousness with which people adopt leisure pursuits, there seems to be little time to stop and worship.

Whether the Christian is at work or participating in the worshipping community, worship is the context for all that he or she does. At work we perceive the hand of God behind everything and through the worship of God's people we discover him afresh. It is not just that worship gives us what we need to face the next week, it also gives us an oportunity to be thankful for all that we have perceived of God throughout the past week. We deprive God of worship not only in the paucity of our corporate worship but by neglecting remembrance of him in our working lives. Worship is the context for service.

Worship and social justice

In Romans 12:1–2 Paul appeals to us,

> . . . by the mercies of God, to present your bodies as a living sacrifice, holy and acceptable to God, which is your spiritual worship. Do not be conformed to this world but be transformed by the renewal of your mind, that you may prove what is the will of God, what is good and acceptable and perfect (RSV).

The context for these familiar verses is worship. Jim Wallis comments that Paul is saying that conformity to this world is more than a failure of lifestyle or politics; *conformity to the world is a failure of worship.*[2]

It is possible for the Christian to think through every conceivable position with 'a Christian mind'; to give away all his resources, and to be heavily involved in politics, and yet reflect only the sterility which can result from a life devoid of worship. It is also possible for a church to build new buildings, to add dance and drama groups, and to change the songs that it sings, yet still to conform to the world in many of the values which it holds dear. How can we say that we worship God if we do not show his character and his kingdom in the church?

We should not be surprised that there is a link between worship and politics, for both ask the questions, 'To whom do we offer our allegiance?' and 'From where do we derive our security?' It is not possible for the Christian to be loyal to God on Sundays and to a political party from Monday to Saturday, for, as Jesus says 'Where your treasure is, there your heart will be also.'[3] We may protest that we worship God, but it may be evident to other people that we do not derive much security from that source.

> If Jesus is Lord, then Caesar is not. If Jesus is Lord then neither mammon nor the nation is the object of worship. If Jesus is Lord, then his disciples have no other laws. In short, worship expresses to whom we belong.[4]

The biblical option for the poor does not express a political preference but is about worship. This is one of the most crucial messages for the contemporary church to convey to secular politicians. When the church speaks out against injustice on behalf of the poor it is not expressing a preference for left-wing politics but is being faithful to the God of justice. The fact that some clergy have publicly expressed an option for left-wing politics has only confused the issue. Whatever their private commitments, it is important that the church is perceived to be articulating a biblical agenda rather than contributing to the see-saw of party politics. It often appears that even the clergy do not perceive that the God of justice makes such stringent ethical demands of his people that any secular political ideology pales into insignificance. To talk frequently and often about poverty and justice is certainly more likely to attract the label 'socialist' than 'Christian'.

Worship has an ethical dimension which cannot be avoided. To privatize worship as we have often done in the past is to weaken its force and challenge in a world which hungers for transcendence.

The worship of Narcissus

The infiltration of the church by narcissism is so important that we must say a little more about it here. Perhaps Christopher Lasch's words will recall something of the anguish of modernity.

> We live in a western world which considers itself to be free from religion but this gap has been replaced by the creed of self-love. Emotional shallowness, fear of intimacy, hypochondria, pseudo-self-insight, promiscuous sexuality and the dread of old age and death, all add up to a frantic search for fulfilment, a therapeutic culture and the world of the resigned.[5]

The problem for narcissists is that they have an inadequate view of themselves and are constantly seeking affirmation in all that they do. Life exists for *them*. If they cannot derive affirmation from it, it may as well not exist. Such a position is fundamentally at odds with the Christian call to be taken up with God in worship. Not only do 'Christian' narcissists concentrate on their own experience of worship (something which is common to many Christians today, as we have seen), but they make their own experience of worship and its intensity one of the indicators of their own experience of God. They literally replace the worship of God with the worship of self, since a good experience of worship is a good experience for themselves. This is purely a 'consumer view' of worship. The narcissist worships to get 'a buzz'.

This can become a form of addiction as, in common with other types of addiction, the person requires ever bigger doses to maintain a constant sense of affirmation. They are likely to employ particular methods of getting themselves into a state of 'awareness' which may have more in common with eastern mysticism than with conventional Christianity. In the final stages they may convince themselves that all manner of things have taken place at the services they have attended, of which other people were not aware.

One element in this need for affirmation is the general anxiety felt by many Christians living against the background of a materialistic society. People without faith place their trust in things that they can see and from which they derive both personal security and social status. The pressure on Christians who worship an invisible God, is to demand that he show himself in some way so as to authenticate their faith. But the basis of Christian behaviour is that we walk by faith and not by sight. To demand that God provide us with miracles and signs to authenticate his existence is to act like those who demanded a sign from Jesus. He replied that they would be given only the sign of his death and resurrection. This does not mean that healings do not take place today, only that we manipulate God when we demand them as our right.

The fact that some of us derive much of our security from material things and are losing our grip on God is evident from the amount of anxiety which Christians currently generate. As we have seen, this anxiety is a sad indication of the presence of narcissism in the church.

Security and sonship

How are Christians to rediscover their security in God? One way would be to rediscover the heart of the gospel which is the spirit of adoption. Paul tells us that our attitude is to be the same as that of Jesus,

> Who, being in very nature God,
> did not consider equality with God
> something to be grasped,
> but made himself nothing,
> taking the very nature of a servant,
> being made in human likeness.
> And being found in appearance as a man,
> he humbled himself
> and became obedient to death –
> even death on a cross!
> Therefore God exalted him to the
> highest place
> and gave him the name that is above
> every name,
> that at the name of Jesus every knee
> should bow,
> in heaven and on earth and under the earth,
> and every tongue confess that Jesus
> Christ is Lord,
> to the glory of God the Father.[6]

It is this spirit of service which Christians seek to emulate whether they are involved in evangelism, social action, or Bible teaching. It is God-motivated and God-centred, and works for the good of others. But how are people to arrive at such freedom if they are terminally anxious and turned in on themselves?

In the life of Jesus this servanthood is most clearly seen when he washes his disciples' feet.[7]

> Jesus knew that the Father had put all things under his power, and that he had come from God and was returning to God; so he got up from the meal, took off his outer clothing, and wrapped a towel round his waist. After that, he began to wash his disciples' feet, drying them with the towel that was wrapped round him.[8]

Jesus is aware of his authority, his identity and his destiny. Firstly, he knew that the Father had put all things 'under his power' and that he had authority even over death. He did not have to prove himself by demonstrating power over people. Secondly, he knew who he was. He had come from God and was accepted by God. He had nothing to prove by acting in a superior manner towards other people. Thirdly, he knew his destiny was to return to the Father. He, therefore, had nothing to prove by currying favour with other people.

Jesus, being secure in his authority, his identity and his destiny was set free from having to prove anything to others. Everything that he was, he was in relation to the Father. *Because he was confident of his status as a Son he was set free to be a servant.*

If narcissism has infiltrated the church with its cult of self-worship and its anxiety, it is because of a problem with worship. We started by saying that worship is God's right. Just before Christ (portrayed as the Lamb) opens the scroll which surely represents God's perspective on human history, a song is sung in heaven.

> 'Worthy is the Lamb, who was slain,
> to receive power and wealth and
> wisdom and strength
> and honour and glory and praise!'[9]

These are all goals that motivate us in our anxious competitive life while on earth. All of human history, which has prompted us to ask 'Why?' of so many events, is driven by the quest for these things. Yet they belong to Christ by right because he committed the ultimate act of selflessness in dying for his enemies on a cross. In worship we acknowledge afresh that the things that cause us to become selfish and which have threatened to drive us throughout the week, actually belong to Christ the Lamb and not to us. He will give these things to those who, as their priority, seek the reign of God and the justice which is its hallmark.

Worship and the gospel

Worship is our joyful response to God on understanding how he has accepted us by his grace and has adopted us as sons and daughters into his family. This grace is free and undeserved. All that we do in Christian service is done out of a grateful remembrance of what God has already done for us.

Yet some Christians do not seem to understand this. They seem still to see Christian service as a duty rather than a joy. They see themselves not as God sees them but as the devil would like them to appear – still in bondage.

All worship is a response to truth. God reveals himself in creation and in the Scriptures and we respond in worship. Worship does not precede revelation as some seem to think. We can worship only what we know. As we have seen, it is important to be committed to all that God has revealed about himself if we are to be sure we are worshipping the true God. Renewal of worship must not start and end in the human heart, but spill over into a motivating force which leads the church out in mission.

Renewal of worship like this will depend on a fresh commitment to the truth which inspires and guides worship. This will involve a recovery of prophetic and expository preaching in particular, so that church congregations everywhere may respond to the Word of God rather than the views of the preacher. Here is the vital link between worship and the gospel, worship and the truth, worship and the Scriptures, which has made the evangelical movement such a potent force for personal and social transformation in the past.

Such a fresh vision of God will bring new energy into the church and will cause people to re-evaluate what they are doing with their time and talents to advance the cause of the kingdom. We must therefore consider the question which faces everyone who has recognized afresh the need for action: 'But what can I do?' In the next chapter we reflect on some of the reasons that some people may feel unable to take any action at all, then we look at how to channel new energy, derived from a fresh glimpse of God, into effective action.

CHAPTER THIRTEEN

BUT WHAT CAN I DO?

Anything for a quiet life.
Don't rock the boat.
TRADITIONAL

I had set out to raise the issue. It has been raised. Part of the achievement of Band Aid was the memory it left of one day of decency in a tawdry world. We had shown that Edmund Burke was right when he said, 'Nobody made a greater mistake than he who did nothing because he could only do a little.' Live Aid had shown that whatever little you could do there was a need for it and it was important that you do something.
BOB GELDOF

Many of us feel powerless to change the world we live in, even though we wish it were different. We adapt to the world and do not expect it to change simply because we have passed through it. After all, one of the main planks of middle-class behaviour is the attempt to get through life 'with the minimum of fuss'.

Yet as we sit night after night in front of our television sets watching global problems unfold which demand a response, it is no wonder that so often we end our evening's viewing feeling weary. The parade of complex need is particularly tiring if we have decided that we can do nothing to change the situation. This assumption too readily condemns us to impotence. It is called 'doing nothing in front of the television'.

All this instant information makes demands on us that we feel are unfair. We resent the fact that the suffering of strangers on the other side of the globe should have the power to make us feel we should respond. At the same time we wish that their situation were different. The needs of strangers intrude into our private lives, which are mostly characterized by a sense of control and orderliness. However we respond, we wish our private lives to remain largely undisturbed.

Sermons too can make demands on us which appear unreasonable. Those who have attended major Christian festivals and conventions, with their numbers of seminars on diverse but equally urgent topics, may be familiar with the numbness and mild panic which can set in. As each speaker challenges us to respond, we begin to wish that we had more lives than the proverbial cat so that we could give one away at each seminar in the service of such pressing need! Members of local churches also have to find ways of coping with the demands made on them from the pulpit. Many a church member has reduced the passionate and all-embracing demands of the preacher to 'take up the cross' to a call to 'support your local church', something which fits in quite neatly to their pattern of normality and is therefore both containable and controllable. It is a defence mechanism, a way of coping and preserving intact our sense of self.

The call to be effectively involved in society, which has been one of the principal themes of this book, could founder on several different counts. Many a notebook has been filled by people who have been moved by the needs they were considering, but who felt neither empowered or enabled to act in any effective way. We have become used to a certain detachment in the way we approach such things. In fact we have become used to separating knowing from doing. This separation is foreign to the biblical way of thinking. In Hebrew to 'know' something is to take responsibility for it and to act on it. As we saw in our discussion of worship, the Israelites had to 'do justice' and not just assent to it if their worship, was to be acceptable to God.

> Biblical faith is not cheap grace or nominal assent because knowing means doing and obedience means faith. You can't divide them. Remove obedience from faith and you have cheap grace. Remove faith from

> obedience and you have legalism. Only where they are inseparable do you have true faith.[1]

So much information is thrown at us in our global village that we are aware of more problems than previous generations ever were. We compare this seeming infinity of problems with our own finite resources and feel helpless. Even if we gave everything away in the cause of Christian compassion it would make no mark on the scale of problems we face. It is easy to come to the conclusion that everything is a hopeless gesture. Yet Christians are called to embody hope and not despair. Our response to problems must be to believe that 'one person plus God is a majority'.

The problems which we face represent a challenge to our own conception of ourselves. For medieval men and women who lived in a smaller and more integrated world, there was more preparation for the choices they faced. Tradition and past experience were a good guide to the present. In our society the pace of change forces us to meet life ill-prepared. We sympathize with Alice when she says, 'One can't believe impossible things.'

'I daresay you haven't had much practice', said the Queen. 'When I was your age I always did it for half an hour a day. Why, sometimes I've believed as many as six impossible things before breakfast.'[2]

The continual need to choose in the face of persistent change can leave individuals not only wondering whether they have any role to play in the world, but also unsure of their own personal identity, since nothing in their past seems to have prepared them for the situations they continually face. *Knowing more* than we can *do* can threaten our personal integrity as well as our social cohesion.

There are three states we need to recognize as we move from a lack of response of any sort, to effective involvement. *Alienation* provides us with a menu of reasons to explain why we do not get involved but remain sitting in our churches fine-tuning church culture. *Participation* presents us with both the problems and the opportunities we find when we begin to get involved. *Anticipation* provides us with the challenge of being contemporary in a fast changing society as well as dealing with the problems of what has come to be called 'future shock'. For it may be that when we decide to get involved as Christians we find that not only are we reacting rather than taking the initiative, but that we are responding to an agenda which is already dated.

Alienation: stranger in a strange land

There are four stages of alienation which Christians may experience when challenged to become involved in the world, or when presented with a set of problems to which they remain passive. These are indifference, introspection, inertia and incompetence.

1. Indifference

To be indifferent is to let nothing make a difference to you. An indifferent person shows no care or concern about anything. He is uninterested in what is going on around him. *An indifferent person cannot, by definition, be a Christian.* The Apostle John says, 'Whoever does not love does not know God for God is love.' This love is of a self-giving kind. It is the very opposite of indifference.

Whether people are indifferent because they are wrapped up in themselves, or simply because they are bored, is of little consequence. A church which is so wrapped in its own problems that it has forgotten the burning need outside is in mortal danger. The church in Laodicea characterized itself as 'rich; I have acquired wealth and do not need a thing'. Yet God was about to judge that church. Indifference and smug self-satisfaction are terrible in anybody, especially in those who call themselves Christians.

2. Introspection

There is a fundamental difference between introspection and meditation. The former is listening to the self, the latter is listening to the Holy Spirit. If we are focused on our selves we will be prey to believing all kinds of things which will put us in bondage. Because we are fallen we have a distorted view of ourselves. We tell ourselves that we are inadequate or that we are grandiose. We justify sinful behaviour. In fact the self is what the Bible calls the 'flesh' or 'the sinful nature'. Paul says in Galatians, 'Live by the Spirit, and you will not gratify the desires of the sinful nature.'[3]

Introspection is not 'quietness' nor is it 'shyness'. It is being focused on self. *The introspective Christian cannot grow spiritually.* Only by focusing on the life and message of the Holy Spirit can people live God's way. Instead of focusing on our own inadequacies the Spirit directs us to live in the light of the adequacy of God.

3. Inertia

According to my dictionary, inertia means 'a disinclination to move or act'. Here too is a serious problem. *The Christian who does not act cannot be obedient.*

Inertia often sets in for two reasons, associated with the presentation of and the response to problems.

Many contemporary issues are presented to individuals as problems which cannot be solved. The demands on our finiteness are so great that we cannot respond. It has often been said that 'the need does not constitute the call', but it is hard to remember that when presented with people dying through poverty. Paralysis is a rational response to overload. We cannot process the information. We are convinced that we have nothing which can change the situation and we often do nothing as a result.

Arising from this is the guilt which goes with such inertia. Ironically, while painfully aware that we can do nothing, we often convince ourselves that nothing will happen if we do not do something about the problem. Since we are not doing anything, we feel guilty. This in turn increases our inertia. So guilty feelings become associated with inaction.

Whatever we do, we must do out of love, joy, thankfulness and the desire to serve. Not out of guilt.

4. Incompetence

Incompetence means that we do not know *how* to put anything into practice. *The incompetent Christian cannot be effective.* But incompetence is the least of our problems of alienation.

There are two sorts of incompetence. 'Innocent' incompetence admits that although it is keen to do the job it does not know how. Everybody who now appears a master of his or her subject was once an innocent incompetent, though they may not wish to be reminded of it! Admitting that we need help is the starting point for all true learning.

The problem comes with the other kind of incompetence. The 'arrogant incompetent' is sure that he does know how things should be done and it is quite painful to try and convince him that he is wrong. Few sights are as painful as the incompetent open-air evangelist who waves a Bible on the most strategic corner of the town square, faithfully putting off hundreds with his incoherent ramblings. These people need strong pastoral discipline, exercised in the hope that God may graciously channel their undoubted energies into more effective service.

But if the desire to learn is there, what is needed is information and training. Firstly, people should be counselled to narrow down their area of interest and start from where they are. For instance, a person who feels interested in overseas aid problems may do better to stay at home and use the social work training she had some years ago. People need guidance to use those human resources which God has already entrusted to them as the basis for their involvement.

Secondly, when we have found the right area of involvement it is relatively simple to find out what is being done by both Christian and secular agencies and to begin to develop in that area.[4] Incompetence can be quickly dispelled if we are humble and willing to learn.

The concept of calling

One of the problems behind alienation is our neglect of the concept of calling. Christ sets us free to follow our calling. He does not taunt us, holding out more to accomplish in our life than we could ever complete. Paul tells us that God does not tempt us with things we are unable to bear.[5] When God calls us he gives us exactly that amount of work to do that befits our talents and our vision. He does not create square pegs and then delight in fitting us into round holes in the name of 'sanctification'. God has created us unique. There is something that we can do which cannot be done by anybody else. This is our calling. It is not an idea which is restricted to the religious sphere or to medical personnel. Each person created by God is created for a reason.

It may well be that God calls us to do only one thing at a time. But to neglect that one thing calls into question what we are here *for*, and places a burden on our fellow Christians because we are not 'covering the base'. As in any joint effort if people are not doing their job then the burden will fall on the conscientious few, who are put under great strain and who have no hope of being able to accomplish a job which was designed for the whole church to undertake.

All too often our way of showing that we are 'real' Christians is to seek to do more. But in these days of 'overload' and 'burnout' we are slowly learning that there is little virtue in volume. What *is* important is to do the right things in the right way. This depends on knowing our calling and its limits. For some people obedience will actually mean 'cutting down'.

> The different spheres of our callings are like a series of concentric circles. We all live at the bull's eye. Now we can go where we don't live, and we can do things even beyond where we can afford to go, such as vote, write letters, or send money. And if we extend our influence

> to the furthest limits, the last limit of all is prayer. We can pray for countries which we will never be able to visit and so on.[6]

Os Guinness continues,

> But at the end of the day, when we reach the limits of the last concentric circle, those limits are not simply a curse. They provide a point of rest and a reminder of our finiteness. And in a fallen world, knowing our finiteness is not only a consequence of sin but a matter of deep rest. 'Sufficient unto the day is the evil thereof.' The Lord alone is sovereign, and we are not. So when we've done all we can, anything beyond that is neither our calling nor our responsibility.[7]

In a world in which we are frequently bewildered about those areas in which we should participate and how we should anticipate a rapidly changing agenda, this is comforting news.

Participation: Christian involvement in society

It is often true that the call to become involved in society is met with a series of groans. People are so busy that they scarcely have time to think let alone take on a whole new agenda. This is why the concept of calling is so important. It reinforces the view that many Christians are already in public life. It asks that we start with what we've already got in terms of resources.

Bringing Christianity to bear on day-to-day business or medical or educational practice can be thoroughly costly but it is an essential part of what is meant by being 'effective'. Whether it is parents who seek to run the home on Christian principles or the manager who is running a plant, it will always be easier to duck the issues and rely on a private faith to 'get through'.

The supportive role of the church

The fact that many teachers, social workers, mothers, accountants, craftspeople and factory workers are struggling each day to live openly for Christ is not acknowledged as it should be. The church betrays itself when it applies the word 'calling' only to religious life and neglects those who are struggling against all odds in the world. All too often the only people who have hands laid on them and who are commissioned to go into the world are conventional missionaries.

Wouldn't it be great if each Sunday a different group was called out to the front and interviewed about what they were facing in their jobs and what their needs were? The church would then gather round and then pray for them, commissioning them to go back into their jobs with renewed commitment. Medics, teachers, mothers and factory workers would all be affirmed and commissioned. Let's demonstrate that we believe in lay calling by recognizing it in our services. Otherwise we might perpetuate the myth that Christianity is a Brahmin culture.

The other side of this is the need to support people who are salt and light in the world. The person who belongs to a trade union and who becomes an official is so often made to feel that because he cannot always attend midweek church meetings, he has backslidden. At the very time when he needs the interest and support of the local prayer meeting he is not getting it. This drives a wedge between those who feel that they must bring a Christian influence to bear on the Trades Union Movement and those who pray.

This must lead us to question some church leaders about the degree of their interest in what their congregation *actually does during the week*. One gets the impression, at least some of the time, that they are so absorbed with their own religious world and are so busy themselves, that they have no time to appreciate some of the strategic work which is going on under their noses. In place of this emphasis on the church's mission in the world, the lay person has to adjust to the religious world of meetings and church buildings.

As society becomes secularized it is no wonder that powerful preaching is on the wane, for clerical preachers are not always in step with their congregations. This deficiency is not only a powerful argument for team ministry. It prompts a plea to the denominations to recognize the importance of lay ministry as equal to but different from clerical ministry. The lay person can be admitted to places where a cleric could never go, just as a cleric is privileged as a pastor to be invited into people's lives at their greatest turning points of birth, marriage and death.

Some clergy do wrestle with contemporary issues, precisely because they are trying to serve the needs of their congregation. They take time and trouble to visit their congregation in their work place as well as at home. They learn about the pressures they are under. Where Christians are actively involved in the community it is often because the preaching and teaching of the Word are equipping people for service effectively.

God leaves us with many questions which we dismiss at our peril. To wrestle with them will lead to growth. No individual who wishes to get involved in the problems of the real world will be able to maintain a 'neat' faith in which all the ends are tied up. Involvement not only raises hard and difficult questions but arouses real grief over the human condition, which may cause the Christian to ask 'Why?' If the church community in which she worships is not prepared to provide the right supportive framework, she may well become disillusioned and either return to the safety of church culture, or, if she persists in her involvement, may run the risk of being ostracized by a church which cannot bear the questions which she is raising. In this sense as well, involvement is costly. It is best done by the whole church and not by factions or individuals. The cost of involvement demands the support and nurture of the whole church.

Social service or social action?

The Grand Rapids Report entitled *Evangelism and Social Responsibility*[8] talks of social responsibility exercised in two ways; social service and social action. These terms roughly describe, first, alleviating the symptoms of distress exhibited in people's lives, and, secondly, removing the causes of those symptoms through wider social action. As the report admits, the two are not independent of each other. The first involves philanthropic activity and the second political and economic activity. The first focuses largely on individuals and families while the second concentrates on structures.

> On the one hand social action of a political kind lacks integrity if it is not supported by a personal commitment to social service. On the other, some works of mercy have inescapably political implications – for example, teaching the oppressed to read and write, visiting a banned person in South Africa, or sending food to Poland or North Vietnam.[9]

Both evangelism and social responsibility are to be sensitive and appropriate in the way they meet human need. Both are necessary but the context may show which is the most appropriate way to demonstrate the gospel. As the African proverb says, 'empty bellies have no ears'.

The mission of the whole church to the whole world is to care for the whole person. Different people and ministries in the body of Christ ensure that different parts of people's needs are met, but all are called to work together to bring about the spiritual and social transformation which can come only through the power of the Spirit.

Our response to this exciting and all-embracing mission parallels that which faced the little boy in the multitude as their need became apparent. Five thousand men, with an unknown number of women and children, were hungry and needed to be fed. It took real courage and no little faith for that boy to believe that what he had was an appropriate thing to offer in the face of such great need. Yet Jesus took just five loaves and two fishes, blessed and broke them, and fed thousands with them.

Faced with the appalling need of our world, it takes a great deal of courage and faith to ask 'What can I do?' It may mean visiting the lonely, debt counselling, marriage counselling, running a soup kitchen, helping at a night shelter, nurturing self-help groups for unemployed people, becoming a foster parent, running a welfare rights centre, becoming a parent governor at the children's school, running a mother and toddler group or teaching English as a foreign language to Bangladeshi women who feel like strangers in a strange land. The possibilities are endless. There is something for everybody to do. As we do it prayerfully in a spirit of Christian service, it is for Jesus to take what we offer and see how many people he can feed with what we bring. He is the one who does the miracles; we are the ones who supply the stuff of which miracles are made.

As we get involved in Christian service we shall quickly realize how vast the issues are. The homeless long for a home. The lonely long for community, the poor long for enough, the unemployed want jobs. We shall often feel that we are scratching the surface of need and that for every person we help, two wait for us to turn to them. We shall see that the causes of their need are not deficiencies in their makeup, but are deeply embedded in the way our society is willing to tolerate such grievous need in its midst. This may well lead us to social action on behalf of those we serve.

In a democracy group pressure is more powerful than individual interest. It is important (and not very costly in terms of time or money) for Christians to support groups which represent the needs of the poor, or fight for the environment. Such groups depend on support. Neither pressure groups campaigning for change nor charities seeking to ameliorate need can function without an active constituency which gives them power by its very support.

Christians who think carefully about their giving might consider how to support financially those organizations which are doing what they themselves have no time to do. So many worthwhile causes are hampered by lack of finance, and it is time for us to realize that we need to think strategically about how we give our money as well as how we commit our time.

Christians need to keep well informed, and one way of doing so is by supporting organizations which take the initiative in national issues. Some have local groups which discuss the issues and take action.

There is, then, no excuse for us to hover on the brink of involvement in society. Inaction is a vote for the *status quo*. Christians are in the business of transforming both the individual and society through the work of the Holy Spirit.

Anticipation: prophetic insight in a fast-changing world

We have already described the effects that increased pluralism can have on the church and society (chapter three). A new phrase was coined in 1970 when sociologist Alvin Toffler published a book entitled *Future Shock* which focused on the *rate* of change in our society. Toffler said that such was the pace of change that it had given rise to 'a new and upsetting psychological disease'. This rising rate of change

> . . .makes reality seem, sometimes, like a kaleidoscope run wild . . . Change is avalanching upon our heads and most people are grotesquely unprepared to cope with it.[10]

French sociologist Raymond Aron once observed that 'Few people are contemporaries of their own generation.' Most of us rely on an education which we received some time ago and that education was itself passing on to us the distilled wisdom of past generations. It did not see its job as enabling us to interpret the future (which is a trifle uncertain at the best of times!).

It is easy for Christians to think that by generally participating in society they are being effective. Unfortunately things are not as easy as that. We are easily wrong-footed by the rapid pace of change in our societies. One can be effective only when one is addressing the right agenda. There is no point in knowing how to answer questions which were answered some time ago to everyone's satisfaction. Christians must learn to anticipate in order to participate.

This again underlines how important it is for Christians to be released and encouraged to stay in the professions. *We need watchmen* – people placed at strategic points so that they can lookout and warn the community in advance of any impending threat. We need people in the forefront of the professions who can tell us, not what is happening now, but what is likely to happen next year or even in the next decade. Christians must learn to be prepared for debates when they occur so that they can participate in them *as* they occur rather than discovering them when they are long dead.

Take the debate over fifth generation computers. One of the ethical questions in the debate about artificial intelligence is, 'If machines can think, what is man?' A debate over the status of thinking raises questions about the nature of consciousness and also about both the origins of mankind and the ability of scientists and technologists to create in their own image. These machines will not only eventually design other computers but they will also program each other. It will soon reach the stage when scientists understand neither the questions nor the answers which computers are posing as they talk to themselves. Here is the ultimate idolatry of man: making something which exhibits a kind of scientific transcendence. Most of us are already in awe of what computers can do, for their operation is a mystery to us.

Or what of the future of *in vitro* fertilization? As the technique advances it will become technically possible to keep fertilized ova alive in the test tube for longer periods. At the same time, paediatric technology is able to keep ever more premature babies alive. Might there not come a point where it is technically possible to fuse the two technologies and keep babies alive from conception to term outside the womb? The questions then will be, 'What is the womb? Who needs it? What is woman; what is man?' It is important that people in that field not only alert society if this 'science fiction' scenario is likely to occur, but that they take a personal stand against such things, for God is the only creator.

Idolatry of things made by one's own powerful techniques is only another instance of the extension of the 'domain of control'. Previously we described this domain as the area over which men and women had *personal* control because of their wealth. Now however it is the *social* domain within which mankind is tempted to say, 'I have done this with my own hand.' We are back to the sin of Babel.

The pace of change technologically is outstripping our ability to think ethically. Because the economic point of view which technology serves has stripped progress of its morality, we are tempted to think that *'possible equals permissible'*. We are constantly being presented with techniques which force us back to retrospective ethical reflection. Had an ethical framework been present from the beginning, some technological developments might never have taken place.

This applies not only to evils such as nuclear warheads. Think of the complexities of medical ethics which have arisen because of the advent of intensive care technology or advanced open-heart surgery. These procedures are good in that they save lives. But intensive care technology poses the problem of when to declare a person dead and switch off the life-support system. We had to develop a new definition of death, brain death, to accommodate the new technological possibilities. And expensive open-heart surgery raises a question about the distribution of health care. For the cost of one heart transplant it may be possible to treat hundreds of other patients who require less expensive remedies. How does one weigh the saving of a single life against the improved quality of life of hundreds?

These problems arise, not only because society is changing fast, but also because technology does not reflect any in-built moral values. We are back to the tyranny of the economic point of view.

Human beings find this fast pace of change so profoundly disturbing because we suspect that the future which is being shaped by technology is not 'human'. Rather, efficiency seems to be the dominant criterion, and humanity serves the machine rather than the other way round.

This being so, the world needs people who are secure in their identity and destiny in God and who can do *something* to make this world more pleasing to him. Whenever we are tempted to give up or to settle down, we must remember that 'nobody made a greater mistake than he who did nothing because he could only do a little'.

CHAPTER FOURTEEN

THROUGH THE NEEDLE'S EYE

I know all about the despair of overcoming chronic temptations. It is not serious provided self-offended petulance, annoyance at breaking records, impatience, etc. don't get the upper hand. No amount of falls will really undo us if we keep on picking ourselves up each time. We shall of course be very muddy and tattered children by the time we reach home. But the bathrooms are all ready, the towels put out, and the clean clothes in the airing cupboard. The only fatal thing is to lose one's temper and give it up. It is when we notice the dirt that God is most present in us; it is the very sign of his presence.

C. S. LEWIS

Individual responsibility has been eroded by therapy, and morality by economics. This state of affairs is responsible for much of the misery in our modern society. Some believe that Christianity itself has become so infiltrated with these ways of thinking that the possibility of its providing any kind of resolution to our problems is now unthinkable. Those of us who opt for it are thought to be taking the 'escapist' way out, by avoiding the problems of our society and hoping they will go away while we immerse ourselves in religious affairs. In an age dominated by science, religion still has the aura of the magical and has been discredited as the foundation for any code by which we might live together as an ethical community.

Morality and moralism

Yet that is the ideal, as David Smail, Professor of Clinical Psychology, insists in the last chapter of his book *Taking Care.*[1]

> It seems altogether likely that human societies are unable to organise themselves without a degree of inequality, and that, therefore, disparities in power are inevitable. The ideal of a just and equal society in which care is taken that every member of it shall be able to develop his or her potentialities to the full, and in which, for example, largely illusory processes of therapy are rendered unnecessary through the ministrations of love, represents an achievement so distant as to be indescribable in any coherent formulation.[2]

Such a society is of course 'indescribable' once one has ruled out the availability of divine power to overcome the bias of self-interest and to replace it by the power of love. Christians know that the church is meant to be that society which exhibits the power of love and to which all who long for 'justice and righteousness' are drawn. But we have been infiltrated by thinking which has debased us.

> The empty shell of a Christian ethics, having for many centuries been laid siege to by the interests of power, has at last been taken over by the values of the market: Christianity becomes simply another way of getting things, achieving 'fulfilment' or a kind of exclusive 'salvation'. Most of us therefore, live in a society in which there is no formal authority, no ethically based, publicly institutionalised code of conduct to which people subscribe in common.[3]

Smail distinguishes between *morality*, a living code of conduct which we would need to invent if it did not exist,[4] and *moralism*, the method by which those with power in society explain away the problems of others as being their own fault. (Poverty is due to laziness, AIDS to promiscuity, *etc.*) He arrives at the same conclusion as this book: that morality has been taken over by economics and that this poses a fundamental threat to our society. In the capitalist context this situation arises from the privatization of morality which leaves public conduct to be governed by the market or the state. One does not have to decide whether public activity is right or wrong since the market is seen as infallible.

For instance, in the case of the market, when 'free' marketeers claim that the market is neutral and amoral they give themselves away by the passion with which they defend it. Words like 'efficiency' and 'cost-effective' are not just technical and scientific expressions of fact, they are part of a statement of faith. To 'believe' in the market is to be free from moral uncertainty. One has a rule for life; a code by which most of life can be sorted and analysed. Of course, defenders of the market would never admit that expressions such as 'cost-effective' have become ethical moral judgments. Smail calls such a denial, inversion.

> Invertedly moral expressions have a secret power which to some extent accounts for their ferocity: we bury in the expression 'cost-effective' an assertion of moral superiority which is at the same time disclaimed and therefore cannot be submitted to ethical discussion. In fact, in supposedly making a purely scientific economic judgement, we assert an invertedly moral judgement which, simply because it is out of sight, makes it impossible for us to ask whether something is right just because it is 'cost-effective'. All forms of discourse or rhetoric which purport to be 'value-free' and yet which attempt to give direction to our lives are riddled with moralistic maxims disguised as matters of fact.[5]

Here then is the final stage of the overthrow of morality by economics. While retaining its claim to be a neutral and scientific language, economics has become the new morality, or, perhaps, the new 'anti-morality'. Because the two worlds are so obviously in conflict we would expect the church to be vociferous in its opposition to this threat to a humane and sustainable world. But it is easy to be deluded into thinking that markets have brought us nothing but blessing in the form of a high standard of living. Thus has the sting of the Christian critique of capitalism been drawn.

Once public morality becomes the preserve of the economic system, the decisions of individuals begin to lose significance. As we have observed, the market is represented as impersonal, and a society dominated by it also becomes impersonal (or rather anti-personal). What individuals long for is to belong to a loving and accepting community. What they find is an impersonal system that rewards people according to a policy of 'You get what you pay for.'

Such a system is a breeding ground for the personal inadequacies on which narcissism breeds. We were made for community and for fellowship, for interdependence and for mutual benefit, for love and acceptance. To be deprived of the common life is to be thrust back on our own resources. We dwell on our worst fears about ourselves; we seek praise and cultivate it. We resort to the addictions of food, drink, drugs, fashion, sex, sport or fantasy, to replace the loves we have lost. We ignore the daily challenge of loving those most unlike ourselves, and in doing so dismiss the means of creating community where formerly there was only loneliness. We seek out those most like ourselves to be our 'mirror' and to reinforce what we already believe.

Society craves a fresh revelation of the love of God and of what it means to live in a loving community. But all too often, far from building people up, Christians are guilty of that moralism which puts them down.

Personal morality and the demonstration of love

Often we confuse moralism with making an impact on our society and 'standing up for what we believe'. There are some whose natural response to reading this book will be to criticize the behaviour of others in the name of Christ. Such moral superiority was not the model which Jesus portrayed. He did not claim his right to be 'above' people but saw himself as the 'friend of sinners'. Although he was the Son of God he was accepted as 'one of us'. Yet he maintained his integrity and never compromised the truth.

We do not have to agree with people in order to love them. The therapeutic or counselling model states that the counsellor should neither agree or disagree with the behaviour of the person he is counselling. It is suggested that he has no right to do so. To state his own beliefs would be to abuse a professional relationship. This kind of model may be appropriate for professional counsellors, but in most relationships mutuality and openness mean that both friends must be free to share their beliefs. Christians can form friendships with those whose lives are very different from their own – for instance, homosexuals living with AIDS – by actively serving their friends, demonstrating love for them in practical ways, and by being at hand when needed. But Christians must not give up their right gently to insist that their friend's homosexual lifestyle is wrong. Practical love crosses boundaries and creates community where there was none. In some cases it may be the only way in which Christian love can be conveyed, as words may easily be misunderstood.

I have written little in this book about poverty in the sense of physical want. Its alleviation has traditionally been seen as one of the strengths of the welfare system. This is less so now that the welfare system is being cut back. But physical deprivation is only one aspect of poverty. To be deprived of the fellowship of equals is another form of poverty and it is this on which I have concentrated in this book. Many groups of people suffer this form of deprivation, and did so in the time of Jesus.

Firstly, minority ethnic groups are denied community not only by personal prejudice but also by racism inherent in 'the system'. Secondly, the elderly are often ignored or 'put away', depriving them of fellowship and love. Thirdly, poor people are often located together in inner-city areas where they can be subjected to exploitation as a group and may share bad conditions. Fourthly, the physically and mentally handicapped, who do not measure up to the dreams of a narcissistic society, are often ignored. Fifthly, despite legislation and many positive social changes, women have not yet been granted equality with men in our society.

This blight in society poses an enormous challenge to the power of love to create community and to demonstrate to the world that its dreams are realizable only through the grace and the power of the Creator-God whom they have rejected.

Home: through the needle's eye

God calls us to be in two places at once. We are to be in the church and in the world. Some Christians try to be in only one place. Those who choose to huddle in the church lose their relevance to those in the world. Those who attempt to be Christians in the world while despising the church lose their spiritual authority for doing what they do.

God has chosen the foolish things of this world to shame the wise. He has chosen the foolishness of the cross and foolishness of the church and has promised that through them he will, by the power of the Holy Spirit, bring about his eternal purposes.

We may feel a sense of failure that we do not do more or do not more faithfully reflect the image of Christ to the world. We may be weak, fearful and beset by temptation, but it is we whom God has chosen to bring about his purposes.

There is no phalanx of super-Christians waiting to be released into the world, no dramatic solutions to the world's problems which will drive atheists to their knees. We are the only ones who can offer real hope to the world, and that will always be the case. As far as God is concerned, we are more than enough. The question is not whether we are adequate but whether we think that God is adequate.

The reason it is so hard for any of us to pass through the needle's eye is that we have so much baggage which we must discard if we are to get through. Only a belief in the adequacy of God and the primacy of love will enable us to do so.

We have seen that the desire to control our material lives can be a substitute for a lack of spiritual security. This lack of identity and of a sense of destiny has lead the 'me generation' to rape the world of consumer goods in a frantic attempt to *be* somebody by *having* more. Because those of us who are reasonably wealthy can control our physical environment, others believe that nothing is wrong. Even some Christians involved in social action have become convinced that the problems of the poor can be solved simply by giving them more material wealth and thus 'balancing out' the money. But the rich are full of all the human neuroses and stresses to which the rest of us succumb. They are anxious people. They know that possessing wealth does not mean that all is well. This is one of the best-kept secrets of our materialistic age, which pretends that wealth is the answer whatever the question.

We have seen that the system of welfare which gives people material handouts, cannot confer that loving acceptance which people crave – a craving that drives our therapeutic culture. Those who are poor still long to be loved, affirmed and drawn into community. They are exluded from the society of the world and long to be included and loved for their own sake. This is the mission of the kingdom. *Both* the rich and the poor long for intimacy and community which reflect the intimacy and community of God and his kingdom. But both must come the way of the needle's eye. It is the common entrance which guarantees equality in the kingdom.

If both rich and poor come the way of the needle's eye, it should be natural for the church to be a community of people who, although very different from one another, have found a new identity, security and destiny in the adequacy of God. A church which fails to demonstrate this shows that Christians are not always all that they claim. How we live in Christ *after* we have become Christians says a great deal about the conditions we thought applied in order to become Christians.

I am not calling upon Christians to write to their MPs or to get out their cheque books (though God alone knows how underfunded Christian organizations are). Those people who turned to this book for detailed instructions on what to *do* will be disappointed.[6] Life is not like that. There is no magic in Christianity, and there are no magical answers.

I am calling us to lay this agenda before God, on our knees, and to pray repeatedly that God would so call us to his service in every area of life, that we might be seen to have faithfully used all that God has given us, faced with the appalling need and the poverty of all responses which do not work out what it means to call Jesus Christ, 'Lord'. If God exists and if our desire to obey him is of supreme importance, he will tell us what to do.

Under the microscope

There are three areas, then, where the behaviour of Christians is under scrutiny today.

1. The adequacy of God

God forbade Israel to worship idols because he alone was adequate. Other nations believed that it was as well to worship several idols, as the power of each was constrained by that of the others. But the Creator God has revealed himself as all that we need. Failure to believe this truth would undermine our confidence in God. We shall still believe that there are 'secular' areas of life outside his practical influence. We know in theory that we are only passing through this world and that we should not be deceived into basing our security on it. Yet in our age more than any we are guilty of doing just that. This is what is sapping the influence of God's people.

At the end of his monumental book *Knowing God*, James Packer has a chapter entitled 'The Adequacy of God'. He asks why we are not like the first-century Christians.

> By being exuberant, unconventional, and uninhibited in living the gospel they turned their world upside down, but you could not accuse us twentieth-century Christians of doing anything like that. Why are we so different? Why, compared with them, do we appear as no more

> than half-way Christians? Whence comes the nervous dithery, take-no-risks mood that mars much of our discipleship? Why are we not free enough from fear and anxiety to allow ourselves to go full stretch in following Christ?[7]

One reason is that we are afraid of the consequences of 'going all the way'. We are filled with half-conscious fears that if we live simply we will be inviting poverty in and that if we reach out to others who are unlike us, we ourselves will be rejected. We fear to act 'meekly' in the world, for it is not 'realistic', and we may be despised for our 'weakness'. We prefer to follow social conventions rather than be distinctive. We do not like people to know that we are different because we are Christians.

> It is these half-conscious fears, this dread of insecurity rather than any deliberate refusal to face the cost of following Christ, which makes us hold back. We feel that the risks of out and out discipleship are too great for us to take. In other words, we are not persuaded of the adequacy of God to provide for all the needs of those who launch out wholeheartedly on to the deep sea of unconventional living in obedience to the call of Christ . . . We are afraid to go all the way in accepting the *authority* of God because of our secret *uncertainty* as to his adequacy to look after us if we do.[8]

The problem is now plain. It is called unbelief. Until we go into our world boldly taking God at his word we can never be that salt and light which we talk about.

At the end of his brilliant essay on justification by faith, Tom Wright says this:

> Because God is love, he has sent his own Son to die for us, and his own Spirit to live in us. Because God is righteous, he declares in the present age that all who believe in the risen Lord Jesus are in the right, that their sins are forgiven. To anxious individuals, to a troubled world, to a divided church and to muddled evangelicalism, the biblical doctrine of justification declares: God is God; trust in him; be glad and rejoice in him; and do not be afraid. God is God: therefore relax.[9]

Those of us who are anxious, uncertain and miserable in our riskless orthodoxy should heed these words.

2. The justice of the kingdom

God cares for us as a community, and we cannot claim a personal right to have the best in life when this would affect the quality of life for others in our community. We have seen that although we have much to be proud of in the inheritance which economics has given us and in the welfare system which has reduced absolute poverty in the West, there is still much that is wrong.

It is the need to care for people in relationships which is important. We have emphasized the kind of poverty which results from exclusion. All of us can seek out people who are on the margins of society and draw them in to loving community. At the same time we need to take political action to make our society more pleasing to God. This unity of personal service and social action cannot be separated from our spirituality as expressed in our life of prayer and in our worship. These all belong together, for we belong not just to a secular society but to the kingdom of Jesus Christ.

If we remain unconvinced that the values of the kingdom of God are meant to be made concrete in this world, we shall continue to prevaricate. Our distinctiveness as a community depends on the degree to which we approximate to the kingdom of God and draw on that for our life. If we continue to look like a cult for the private worship of yet another god in our pluralistic society, those who are searching for meaning may well pass us by and go to some other cult. It is when Christianity audaciously claims to have something authoritative to say to the whole of our society that the fireworks begin. We have been damp squibs for too long!

3. The primacy of love

John Stott has said, 'What love desires, justice demands.' It is important that we have a renascence of *agapē* love. We have seen how much of modern Christianity is a search for experience asssociated with our need to feel the presence of God. But *agapē* love is self-forgetful and derives its model from the servanthood of Christ. So it is free to love others.

We need a celebration of love in our tawdry world. We need people whose lives are examples of love in service and who can inspire our young people for good rather than evil. We need to show that Christian love crosses those boundaries which still exist between people. Our world needs to be astonished by love rather than sickened by evil.

This reversal of the world's values can take place only when we realize that acknowledging the Lordship of Jesus Christ in a disobedient world is costly. As for the church, we shall always be a monument to the tireless grace of God. He is willing and able to bring his eternal purposes to fruition using our feeble efforts rather than bypassing us and shaping history without us. If we are fully to demonstrate what it means to be the people of God, we must rediscover the adequacy of God, the justice of the kingdom and the primacy of love. These are reckoned as sheer foolishness in our materialistic world. They will involve us in great risks and much heartache. But in rediscovering them we shall begin to close the credibility gap between what Jesus called his disciples to be and what we have become.

NOTES

Chapter 1

1. Abraham Heschel, *The Prophets* (Harper and Row, 1962), p. 172.

Chapter 2

1. Romans 1:19.
2. Romans 1:20.
3. Romans 1:21b–23.
4. Romans 1:25.
5. Isaiah 44:19–20.
6. Isaiah 44:18.
7. Ray S. Anderson, *On Being Human* (Eerdmans, 1982), p. 95.
8. David Lyon, *The Steeple's Shadow* (IVP, 1986), p. 101.
9. J. A. Walter, *All You Love is Need* (*Third Way*/SPCK, 1985), p. 16.
10. Ezekiel 33:30–32.
11. Susan Sontag, 'Piety without Content' in *Against Interpretation* (André Deutsch, 1987), p. 249.
12. Lesslie Newbigin, *The Other Side of 1984* (SPCK, 1983), pp. 9–10.
13. Charles Taylor, 'In Conversation' (with Michael Ignatieff), *The Listener* (BBC, 1987).
14. Exodus 33:16–17.
15. Peter L. Berger, *Facing up to Modernity* (Penguin, 1979), p. 221.
16. *Ibid.*, p. 222.
17. Os Guinness, *The Gravedigger File* (Hodder and Stoughton, 1983).

Chapter 3

1. I am very grateful to James MacGibbon, the executor of Stevie Smith's estate, for his helpfulness, and for permission to use this poem, which is taken from the Penguin edition of *The Collected Poems of Stevie Smith* (1985), p. 303.
2. Matthew 16:24–26.
3. Paul C. Vitz, *Psychology as Religion: The Cult of Self Worship* (Lion, 1977).
4. Richard Sennett, *The Fall of Public Man* (Faber and Faber, 1986), p. 8.
5. Herbert Hendin, *The Age of Sensation* (New York, Norton, 1975), p. 6. Quoted in Paul C. Vitz, *op. cit.*, pp. 115–116.
6. Christopher Lasch, *The Culture of Narcissism* (Abacus, 1980), p. 7.
7. *Ibid.*, p. 8.
8. *Ibid.*, p. 8.
9. *Ibid.*, p. 225.

10. Vitz, *op. cit.*, p. 120.
11. Kenneth Keniston, *et al*, *All Our Children: The American Family Under Pressure* (New York: Harcourt Brace Jovanovich, 1977).
12. Os Guinness, *The Gravedigger File* (Hodder and Stoughton, 1983), p. 85.
13. For a very helpful discussion of the development of the narcissistic personality in a Christian context see Constance Lawrence 'An Integrated Spiritual and Psychological Growth Model in the Treatment of Narcissism', in *Journal of Psychology and Theology* (1987), Vol. 15, No. 3, pp. 205–213. There is a response to this paper in James D. Guy 'A Reaction to Lawrence', *Journal of Psychology and Theology* (1987), Vol. 15, No. 3, pp. 214–215 and a rejoinder by Lawrence in 'A Response to Guy', *Journal of Psychology and Theology* (1987), Vol. 15, No. 3, pp. 216–217. See also Lee R. Greenlee Jr 'Kohut's Self Psychology and Theory of Narcissism: Some Implications regarding the Fall and Restoration of Humanity', in *Journal of Psychology and Theology* (1986), Vol. 14, No. 2, pp. 110–116. Kohut's main works on narcissism which are foundational to any Christian assessment of the subject, are H. Kohut, *The Analysis of the Self* (New York: International Universities Press, 1971), and *The Restoration of the Self* (New York: International Universities Press, 1977). Two other important books which are more accessible to the lay person are A. Wallach and L. Wallach, *Psychology's Sanction for Selfishness: The Rrror of Egoism in Theory and Therapy* (San Francisco: W. H. Freeman & Co., 1983), and Paul C. Vitz, *Psychology as Religion: The Cult of Self-Worship* (Lion, 2nd edition 1981). See also the review of Wallach and Wallach in Stanton L. Jones, 'Selfish to the Core', in *Journal of Psychology and Theology* Vol. 14, No. 1 (1986), pp. 71–72.
14. Geoffrey Gorer, *The American People: A Study in National Character* (New York: Norton, 1984), p. 74.
15. Beata Rank, 'Adaptation of the Psychoanalytical Technique for the Treatment of Young Children with Atypical Development', *American Journal of Orthopsychiatry*, 19 (1949), pp. 131–132.
16. Andy Warhol, *The Philosophy of Andy Warhol* (New York: Harcourt Brace Jovanovich, 1975), pp. 48–49.
17. Roy Clements, 'The Cult of Narcissus' in the lecture series *Idols of our Time* (two lectures given at the Christian Impact Centre, Vere St., London). This quote is from lecture 1 subtitled *My Right to Inner Security?* I would like to recommend these lectures, obtainable on tape, to anybody interested in a Christian analysis of narcissism. I am indebted to them for many of the insights in this chapter.
18. *Ibid.*

Chapter 4

1. G. S. Becker, *A Treatise on the Family* (Chicago, 1975); see also 'A Theory of Marriage', *Journal of Political Economy* (July/August 1973 and March/April 1974).
2. Adam Smith, *An Inquiry into the Nature and Causes of the Wealth of Nations*, ed. E. Cannan (London, 1904), i. 16, 419. See also *ibid.*, 421 and ii. 43.
3. *Ibid.*

4. Robert Heilbronner, *The Worldly Philosophers* (Simon and Schuster, 1972, 4th edition), p. 18.
5. D. P. O'Brien, *The Classical Economists* (Oxford, 1978), p. 31.
6. F. A. Hayek, 'The Moral Element in Free Enterprise', in *Studies in Philosophy, Politics and Economics* (Routledge and Kegan Paul, 1967), p. 229.
7. Irving Kristol, 'The Disaffection from Capitalism' in *Capitalism and Socialism: A Theological Inquiry*, ed. Michael Novak (American Enterprise Institute, 1979), p. 16.
8. Norman Barry, 'Understanding the Market' in *The State of the Market*, ed. M. Loney *et al.* (Sage, 1988), p. 161. We shall return to the theme of altruism and the size of the community in a later chapter.
9. Brian Griffiths, *The Creation of Wealth* (Hodder and Stoughton, 1984), p. 68.
10. *Ibid.*, pp. 122–123.
11. Fred Hirsch, *The Social Limits to Growth* (Routledge and Kegan Paul, 1977).
12. A. W. Coates, ed., *The Classical Economists and Economic Policy* (Methuen, 1971), p. 9.
13. John Maynard Keynes, 'The Economic Possibilities for our Grandchildren', in *Essays in Persuasion* (Macmillan, 1972), Vol. ix of *The Collected Works of J. M. Keynes*, ed. D. Moggridge.
14. E. F. Schumacher, *Small is Beautiful* (Abacus, 1974), p. 34.
15. W. Temple, *Christianity and the Social Order* (SPCK, 1976), p. 32.
16. *Ibid.*
17. Ayn Rand, *The Fountainhead* (Bantam, 1943). I am grateful to Roy Clements for this quote.
18. Luke 6:32–35a.

Chapter 5

1. *Cf.* Deuteronomy 24:17–22.
2. Isaiah 5:8, RSV.
3. Job 31:13–15.
4. *Cf.* Deuteronomy 24:18.
5. Luke 4:18–22.
6. Nicholas Wolterstorff, *The Bible and Economics: What does it tell us?* Paper delivered at the Oxford Conference on the Christian Faith and Economics (7 January, 1987), p. 7.
7. Roger Scruton, *The Meaning of Conservatism* (Pelican Books, 1980), p. 183.
8. Quoted in Tony Walters, *Fair Shares* (Handsel Press, 1986), p. 98.
9. Bryan Gould, *Socialism and Freedom* (Macmillan, 1985), pp. 8–9.
10. Michael Harrington, *The Other America* (Basic Books, 1980), p. 102.
11. Julian Le Grand, *The Strategy of Equality* (Allen and Unwin, 1982), p. 150.
12. Gould, *op cit.*, p. 61.
13. Brian Abel-Smith, 'Whose Welfare State?', in N. McKenzie (ed.), *Convictions* (McGibbon, 1958), pp. 55–73 (quotation from pp. 55–56).

14. Those who would like to cover the evidence regarding equality as a measure of performance, will find it in my *Ethical Tensions in the Welfare State* (Grove, 1988), pp. 13–14. Indeed the arguments of this chapter generally are expanded there.
15. Roy Hattersley, *Choose Freedom* (Penguin, 1987), p. 23.
16. R. H. Tawney, 'Poverty as an Industrial Problem', in *Memorandum on the Problem of Poverty* (William Morris Press, 1913).
17. For a more extensive distinction between civil rights and welfare rights see Roy McCloughry, *op. cit.*
18. Lesslie Newbigin, *The Welfare State – A Christian Perspective* (Oxford Institute for Church and Society, 1985).
19. *Ibid.*
20. See J. Philip Wogaman, *Towards a Christian Definition of Justice* (paper given at the Regional Conference on Economics and Christianity, Wheaton College, 24 – 25 February, 1989).
21. Julian Le Grand, *The Strategy of Equality* (Allen and Unwin, 1982), p. 151.
22. Michael Ignatieff, *The Needs of Strangers* (Chatto, 1984).
23. *Ibid.*, p. 10.
24. *Ibid.*, p. 11.
25. *Ibid.*, p. 16, emphasis mine.
26. *Ibid.*, p. 19.

Chapter 6

1. Christopher Wright, *Living as the People of God* (IVP, 1983).
2. *Ibid.*, p. 134.
3. Stephen Charles Mott, *Biblical Ethics and Social Change* (OUP, 1982, p. 59).
4. Psalm 146:7–9.
5. Proverbs 17:5a.
6. Nicholas Wolterstorff, 'Why Care about Justice?' in *The Reformed Journal* (Eerdmans, Vol. 36, no. 8). Reprinted in *Third Way* (November, 1987), pp. 21–25.
7. *Ibid.*, p. 23.
8. *Cf.* Mott, *op. cit.*, p. 63ff.
9. Deuteronomy 10:18–19.
10. Job 31:13–15.
11. Wright, *op. cit.*, p. 139.
12. *Cf.* Hosea, 4:1ff.
13. Mott, *op. cit.*, p. 65.
14. Wright, *op. cit.*, p. 197.
15. *Ibid.*, pp. 197–198.

Chapter 7

1. Martin Luther King, *Stride Towards Freedom* (New York, 1958).
2. Exodus, 6 – 12.
3. *Cf.* Daniel 3:18.

4. *Cf.* Daniel 6:13.
5. Acts 4:19–20.
6. Reinhold Neibuhr, *The Children of Light and the Children of Darkness* (SCM, 1944).
7. For this reason I am cautious about the usefulness of Christian parties. Christians are still prone to schism and the prospect of a splinter party from such a Christian party is appalling. If one accepts that different points of view can exist between Christians then why should Christian influence not permeate all parties?
8. Richard John Neuhaus, *The Naked Public Square* (Eerdmans, 1984), p. 116.
9. *Ibid.*, pp. 124–125.
10. William T. Bluhm, *Theories of the Political System: Classics of Political Thought and Modern Political Analysis* (Prentice-Hall, 1978), p. 8.
11. Michael Ignatieff, 'Time to Take New Political Bearings', *The Listener* (BBC, May 1986), p. 16.
12. Neuhaus, *op. cit.*, p. 117.
13. *Ibid.*, p. 114.
14. Matthew 19:8.
15. Oliver O'Donovan, *Resurrection and Moral Order* (IVP, 1986), p. 130.
16. The question of how we respond to this challenge is left to the discussion of personal calling in chapter thirteen.

Chapter 8

1. Woody Allen, *Without Feathers* (Sphere, 1979), pp. 5–6.
2. Romans 12:2.
3. 1 Peter 3:15.
4. 1 Peter 1:13.
5. 1 Corinthians 14:20.
6. Matthew 22:37 (my emphasis).
7. Revelation 18:5.
8. Space precludes a discussion here of Paul's account of the fall in Romans 1:18–32. However, this is his account of the universal fall and those wishing to have a more complete picture should study it closely.
9. Revelation 5:12.
10. Psalm 116:6.

Chapter 9

1. Matthew 11:4–5.
2. Jim Wallis, *The Call to Conversion* (Lion, 1981), p. 12.
3. Matthew 13:44.
4. Matthew 6:10, RSV.
5. Stephen Mott, *Biblical Ethics and Social Change* (Oxford University Press, 1982), pp. 104–105.
6. Graham Cray, 'The Theology of the Kingdom', *Transformation* (Autumn, 1988).
7. *Ibid.*

8. Psalm 89:14.
9. Amos 5:24
10. Graham Cray, *op. cit.*
11. Luke 1:32.
12. Luke 1:52–53.
13. Graham Cray, *op. cit.*
14. Luke 19:9.
15. Erich Fromm, *The Sane Society* (Rinehart, 1955), p. 264. Quoted in Stephen Mott, *op. cit.*, p. 111–112.
16. Ronald J. Sider. Review of *The Evangelical Renaissance* by Donald G. Bloesch in *Christianity Today*, 18 (1974), p. 1161. Quoted in Stephen Mott, *op. cit.*

Chapter 10

1. Kenneth E. Hagin, *How God taught me about prosperity* (Faith Library Publications, 1982).
2. *Ibid.*, p. 22.
3. Luke 12:15.
4. Matthew 5:16.
5. J. A. Walter, *All You Love is Need* (*Third Way*/SPCK, 1985), p. 24.
6. *Ibid.* p. 25.
7. *Ibid.* p. 26.
8. For a very good essay on freedom and human addiction *cf.* William Lenters, *The Freedom we Crave: Addiction the Human Condition* (Hodder and Stoughton, 1980), p. 70.
9. Richard Foster, *Celebration of Discipline: The Path to Spiritual Growth* (Hodder and Stoughton, 1980), p. 70.
10. John 21:22.
11. John 10:10.
12. Tom Sine, *The Mustard Seed Conspiracy* (Word Books, 1981), p. 112.
13. Ezekiel 33:31–33, GNB.
14. Paul Vitz points out that we should also include the Ph.D in this definition! Anybody who has a great deal of this world's assets *in whatever form* is in danger of placing his or her trust and confidence in them rather than God.
15. Proverbs 30:8b–9.
16. Proverbs 11:4.
17. Lenters, *op. cit.*, p. 16.
18. Robert H. Franks, *Choosing the Right Pond: Human Behaviour and the Quest for Status* (Oxford University Press, 1985), p. 9.
19. Quoted in *ibid.*, p. 5.
20. E. F. Schumacher, *Good Work* (Abacus, 1980), p. 26.
21. Richard Layard, 'Human Satisfactions and Public Policy', *The Economic Journal*, 90 (1980), pp. 737–750. This quote is from p. 741.

Chapter 11

1. Richard Lovelace, *Dynamics of Spiritual Life* (Paternoster, 1981), p. 355.

2. Kenneth Leech, *The Social God* (Sheldon Press, 1981); *True Spirituality* (Sheldon Press, 1980); 'Solitude and Solidarity', in *Grassroots* (Part 1, July/August, 1983; Part 2, Sept./October, 1983).
3. Kenneth Leech, 'Solitude and Solidarity'.
4. *Ibid.*, p. 5.
5. On listening see the helpful Grove booklet by Michael Mitton, *The Wisdom to Listen* (Grove Books, Pastoral Series No. 1).
6. Richard Lovelace, *op. cit.*, p. 392.
7. *Ibid.*
8. Stephen C. Mott, *Biblical Ethics and Social Change* (Oxford University Press, 1982), p. 22.
9. Jane Hatfield, *Creative Prayer* (Grove Books, Spirituality Series, No. 7).
10. Jacques Ellul, *Prayer and Modern Man* (Seabury Press, 1973). pp. 76–77.
11. Charles Eliot has written lucidly and with great insight about the relationship between prayer and social issues in *Praying the Kingdom: Towards a Political Spirituality* (DLT, 1985), as has Gerard Hughes in his *God of Surprises* (DLT, 1985); Mark Mills-Powell writes about prayer and nuclear holocaust in *Praying in the Shadow of the Bomb* (Grove Books, Spirituality Series, No. 11); Paul S. Rees has contributed an article entitled 'Prayer and Social Concern' in *The Chicago Declaration*, ed. Ron Sider (Creation House, 1974); Howard Snyder writes on prayer and social concern in his book *Liberating the Church* (Marshalls, 1983); Peter Price has also written on *Prayer and Politics* (*Grassroots*, May/June, 1983).

Chapter 12

1. *Cf.* Jurgen Moltmann, *The Church in the Power of the Spirit* (SCM, 1977), p. 265–267.
2. Jim Wallis, *The Call to Conversion* (Lion, 1981), p. 141.
3. Matthew 6:21.
4. Jim Wallis, *op. cit.*, p. 143.
5. Christopher Lasch, *The Culture of Narcissism* (Abacus, 1979), p. 204.
6. Philippians 2:5–11.
7. John 13:1–17.
8. John 13:3–5.
9. Revelation 5:12.

Chapter 13

1. Os Guinness, 'Knowing And Doing: A Challenge to Think Christianly', in *Radix* (Winter, 1987), p. 6.
2. Lewis Carrol, *Alice Through the Looking Glass* (Thomas Nelson and Sons, this edition undated), p. 75.
3. Galatians, 5:16.
4. I intended to include an appendix to this book, giving guidance on the practical possibilities for taking action in the modern world. It grew and grew until it became a separate book. It is published as *Taking action* (Frameworks, 1990). It contains many examples, names, addresses and

practical suggestions. It is meant to earth the message of the present book in practical action.

5. 1 Corinthians 10:13.

6. Os Guinness, *op. cit.*, p. 28.

7. *Ibid.*

8. *Evangelism and Social Responsibility: An Evangelical Commitment* published by Paternoster Press (1982) for the Lausanne Committee for World Evangelisation and the World Evangelical Fellowship.

9. *Ibid.*, p. 44.

10. For more ideas see my *Taking action* (Frameworks, 1990) and Fran Beckett, *Called to Action* (Collins, 1989).

11. Alvin Toffler, *Future Shock* (Pan, 1973).

Chapter 14

1. David Smail, *Taking Care* (Dent, 1987).

2. *Ibid.*, pp. 150–151.

3. *Ibid.*, p. 143.

4. '. . . unless morality is rescued from its obscurity – what is even almost a state of ignominy – and reinstated at the centre of our public life, it is hard to see how we can begin to construct a society worth living in.' Smail, *op. cit.*, p. 144.

5. *Ibid.*, pp. 146–147.

6. I do give lots of ideas about *what to do* in another book which has another purpose. See *Taking action* (Frameworks, 1990).

7. James Packer, *Knowing God* (Hodder and Stoughton, 1973), p. 303.

8. *Ibid.*, p. 304.

9. Tom Wright, 'Justification: The Biblical Basis and its Relevance for Contemporary Evangelicalism' in *The Great Acquittal: Justification by Faith and Current Christian Thought*, ed. Wright *et al.* (Fount, 1980), p. 37.